FAITH WORKS

FAITH WORKS

A True Story of Radical Obedience

ELEEN VINCENT

iUniverse LLC
Bloomington

Faith Works
A True Story of Radical Obedience

iUniverse books may be ordered through booksellers or by contacting:

iUniverse LLC
1663 Liberty Drive
Bloomington, IN 47403
www.iuniverse.com
1-800-Authors (1-800-288-4677)

ISBN: 978-1-4917-0162-1 (sc)
ISBN: 978-1-4917-0164-5 (hc)
ISBN: 978-1-4917-0163-8 (ebk)

Library of Congress Control Number: 2013914318

Printed in the United States of America

iUniverse rev. date: 09/10/2013

CONTENTS

DEDICATION

Without a doubt this book has to be dedicated to our wonderful children who walked with us through the years of our trials. Rachel, Duncan and David grew up in an environment of faith and sacrifice where at times it must have felt, from their perspective, that they were being sacrificed.

I honor each of them for their obedient walk with the Lord that continues into their adult lives and marriages. With their spouses they have trained their children in the same faith principles that endorse their heritage. May this book bless them. As they recall some of the events, may they not remember the pain that they endured but look back with thankfulness to God who has been faithful to us as a family.

I also wish to dedicate this book to the new generation of faith-filled adventurers who are ready to obey God's call and forsake the normal to do the extraordinary.

ACKNOWLEDGEMENTS

My husband Alan was always there as an encouragement, he believed I could write this book. I thank him for trusting me to tell our story from my perspective. And thank you Natalie Hardy for your advice and many hours of careful editing. You walked every step of the way with me; your skill was invaluable. Whatever the challenge and whatever the need, you have always been there. My thanks also go to Irene Gallagher for her meticulous assistance in so many details. I don't think **Faith Works** would have been written without Karen Elliott's tireless prodding and encouragement. You made me believe it was possible. My granddaughter Emily Vincent helped with ideas for the cover. Together you have been a tremendous help in creating a very presentable and readable book. Thank you!

I have no allusions: **Faith Works** is in your hands today, first and foremost, because of the boundless grace of God. I give Him my thanks.

ENDORSEMENTS

It has been said that everybody loves a good story. Well this is an absolutely great story! *Faith Works: A True Story of Radical Obedience* is well written and very captivating. My wife Cheryl and I both laughed and cried at points. It will inspire many just as the biographies of famous missionaries have done. I can't wait to get this book into the hands of our younger folk as it will be a real inspiration. More than that, it will build your faith and encourage you to persevere regardless of your age. It is the record of the conquests of faith and courage of my favorite couple, told in a way that will fascinate you and make you want to read it right through to the finish. Anyone finding their way through life and those looking for inspiration to finish well will all enjoy Eileen's story. Thanks for writing this.

> **BARRY WISSLER**—*Senior Pastor, Ephrata Community Church; apostolic leader of HarvestNET, International and Outpouring Family International.*

This book is a life-story that will make you cry! It will also make you wonder—what am I willing to risk for God? It is amazing to have parents who have lived a "laid down life" for Jesus. Their passion for God is contagious and ruins you for normality—so beware!

> **RACHEL HICKSON**—*Rachel is the founder of HeartCry for Change, a powerful preacher, author and teacher with an international ministry, and the author's daughter.*

I love what I have read in this book. Wonderful! For anyone who loves adventure, this is your book. Travel, risk taking, and amazing provision as Eileen and her husband head for India. I met them in Bombay years ago and saw sacrifice and huge reward. Faith works! Read this book for yourself, to your kids and grandkids, and grow in your trust of God for great things in your journey with Him.

> **FLOYD MCCLUNG**—*A leader with Youth With a Mission for twenty years, author and minister now living in Cape Town SA.*

Eileen Vincent's new book *Faith Works* should be read by every believer in Christ. When I began to read the manuscript, I found it hard to put down. *Faith Works* is filled with principles of faith written with transparency from true life stories that I found to be so refreshing. These principles of faith have become foundational in Eileen's life, and will become foundational in your life also as you read this amazing story of faith. The stories and truth found on the pages of this book will give you hope and unlock the treasures of faith in your life that will position you for radical obedience to the Lord. Eileen and Alan Vincent have a story to tell that millions need to hear, and this book serves as a tool for this to become a reality. The biblical truth found in this book will transform your life. I love this book!

> **LARRY KREIDER**—*International Director of DOVE International and author of over thirty books.*

FOREWORD

My precious wife Eileen has written a wonderful book that is so readable. She captures our story with pathos, excitement and deep spiritual application. Many of the stories, so familiar to me came alive as I read and I was surprised how deeply I was moved. Eileen teaches profound truths with great clarity and simplicity. It's the kind of book you can give to anyone, whether a young person, a seminary student, or mature professor, pastor or businessman. I only wish that such a book had been available to me when I first got saved. It would have greatly accelerated my spiritual growth. I urge you to read this book prayerfully with the willingness to pay the price to be trained to become a warrior of faith that God can use.

Alan Vincent, an apostolic father and veteran of the faith.

PREFACE

This is the very personal story of two young, idealistic, sold out Christians who just believed that God would do whatever He said He would do. It is Alan's story as well as mine, but told from my perspective. Here, true incidents and impressions of life in India are woven together to create a close up view of faith and radical obedience. The foundation of this book is a manuscript written in 1970, plus hundreds of prayer letters and personal letters written to family during those India years.

As I read what I had written in 1970, certain parts shocked me and I said to myself, *"Eileen how could you think that? Or, how could you behave like that!"* But I have decided to let it stand as it is. The most devastating instances to me were some of my responses to the Lord in prayer concerning His seeming failure. I was ashamed that I expressed such attitudes; but I have decided to leave it and to let you read the honest words of a passionate young woman, who was not always wise. It is as it is. You will see how God did speak to us and wonderfully guide and provide despite my immaturity and obvious spiritual need.

It is a true story of our journey into a life of faith. Here you read of the struggles and the pain that the Lord took us through and today are the foundation of Alan's revelation of faith that he has written about in his books. In one sense this is a book concerning our whole family. Our children were an intimate part of all our adventures. We were confronted to trust God with them when our flesh cried out to protect and keep them with us. Some of those decisions were the hardest, but God is faithful in all these things.

This book is a testimony of how God can use those who do not qualify. I have always considered I was the last person to ever be used by God.

It is a book of how to grow in faith; it underlines the basic necessity of being filled with the Holy Spirit. It tells of the passion for missions; the seemingly reckless behavior of those who will obey the Lord, when their actions are judged as irresponsible or even foolish. It challenges the complacent, fearful, worldly church to hear God and then do what He says. It confronts the "small God" of the western Church. My God is a big God. He is the King of Kings and The Eternal, Glorious, Magnificent One, The Coming One who rules all creation. He chases after His word to do it. He cannot fail and nothing is impossible to Him!

A new missionary thrust is going to the ends of the earth and today many indigenous people are busy obeying the great commission with huge success. You may not have to cross the seas to accomplish God's will and obey the call. Today the streets of our cities cry out for compassion, deliverance, salvation and healing. Will the western church hear the call? Our mission field is all about us. The power of God is here to supply all our needs and He will manifest Himself right in the streets of our cities just as in some far flung place on the map if we come in faith.

Today the danger of persecution for righteousness is right here in our western society. We never dreamed this would happen. It is a wakeup call for the church to rise to the kind of faith that made the apostles say, "Judge for yourselves whether it is right in God's sight to obey you rather than God" Acts 4:19. Let this book encourage you to new levels of faith for health, provision and for all the affairs of family and life. May ***Faith Works: A True Story of Radical Obedience*** get under the 'rational skin' of today's believers and produce a kingdom of faith-filled warriors who will sacrifice everything to follow the Lord and so be His trusted servants in these demanding days. Let the Church know without a doubt, "Those who believe will not be put to shame" and "What is impossible with man is possible with God."

Eileen Vincent

AUTHOR'S NOTE

Bombay: 1970

This book is set in India 1963-1976. The nation we knew then is not what it is today. Bombay, now Mumbai, is a western looking city with over twenty million people and still growing.

The following graphic picture of the Bombay we knew, written from true life situations in 1970, is included here so as to draw you into the heart and reality of the city that became our home. Throughout the book I have called modern Mumbai, Bombay, the name that was so familiar to us.

Milling crowds pushing and elbowing, others aimlessly ambling and shuffling, the noise of street traders calling their wares, the din of traffic and the continuous hubbub of voices all raised to be heard above the yells of children, the pleas of beggars, the fights, the quarrels, the dogs and the sobs. This is Bombay, a city without a heart, a city that would break your heart. Here 6 million people live crammed into tenement houses without privacy, running water or sanitation. Or if they are not so fortunate, they live in abject poverty in shacks on waste ground, swamps and along the road sides cooking, bathing, living and dying in the full view of all who pass by.

A mother came from the hospital with her three-day-old baby to sleep on the pavement in drenching monotonous monsoon rain. Mothers have no satisfaction in seeing their emaciated half-starved babies grow; they are soon bitten by mosquitoes or infected with hook worm which cause small children to have grotesquely swollen abdomens. Many suffer with dysentery and drag their sick bodies through one day to the next.

With anguish, despair and hopelessness the crowds exist wondering what each day is for, as their daily experience is disease and misery.

Then you see a shining new imported car; sitting inside behind the darkened windows are the rich. They glide through the areas of poverty and stench in their air conditioned limousines with perfumed handkerchiefs to their noses, untouched by the painful reality of life for the majority. They live in luxurious apartments, and in complete idleness pass their days being waited upon by numerous servants.

Middle class families struggle to give their children a good education. They sacrifice to send them to college so as to increase their chance of making a living or marrying well. This investment in the next generation is essential so that the parents can be provided for in retirement. But the young graduate only leaves college to join the thousands upon thousands of frantic job searching young people. A successful medical student happily puts a new nameplate on her door, but eventually accepts the only job available, working all hours of the day and night at seven pounds per month in a poor class private nursing home. She is thankful that train travel is cheap, but as the train draws into the station already crammed and overflowing with men hanging all over the outside, she decides to wait for the next train. But the next and the next will be the same. She will have to learn to behave like the crowd; put her head down and push in the unclean crush of hot sweaty bodies where the professional pick pocket maneuvers his hand and makes a good haul.

Looking about, one would think the land was God forsaken. Everywhere, Hindu gods are worshipped. Indians are very religious. On the beach innocent children play in the sand, but a large woman comes down to the sea at sunset with far more serious intent. She wades out into the water quite unconcerned about wetting her sari, and from cupped hands she sips the water then lets it drop back into the ocean. She throws some small coins and flowers into the sea paying homage to a Hindu god; she then turns back to the beach as the sun dips over the horizon turning everything to liquid gold.

The wail goes up from the mosque calling the religious Muslim to prayer. Men unable to get inside the mosque for evening prayer stand in an indescribably filthy, narrow road and then bow in solemn orderly rows with their heads covered. With ardent devotion they come by the thousands to call upon Allah. The traffic respectfully inches past, totally reconciled to the fact that religion has priority even on the roads.

It is said that Bombay is the most civilized and western looking city in India. On getting into the last compartment of a city-bound suburban electric train, one is suddenly transported to a Hindu temple. There in the compartment an idol is set up and six men with cymbals clash them in feverish tempo while one dances frantically with sweat pouring from his body having energy and powers of endurance supplied by the devil. Another man is transfixed like a statue in adoration and worship of the idol. The whole atmosphere is filled with a chilling sense of evil. All the time the train rattles on taking men to insurance offices, banks, law courts, electronics and plastic factories and other places of sophisticated employment.

Here in Bombay you can also meet with Christians and it is the same as meeting with them anywhere in the world. You feel at home. There is love, joy and peace and it is easy to forget the world outside. Once, while sitting among the praising, rejoicing people of God, I saw Bombay like a huge pulsating heart. With every pulse beat the heart moved violently. These were not life throbbing pulse beats but great sobs which wracked the heart. They were the sobs of the mother drenched on the pavement with her three-day-old baby, the sobs of lepers, the maniac and the devil possessed, the sick, the dying, the unemployed, and the hungry. They were the sobs of a city that is lost, of a people without God and without hope in this world. These great heart-broken sobs pressed in upon our meeting place till it seemed as if the very walls were pulsating in unison with this great heart. Yet the walls were a division; inside love, joy and peace—outside a hell. It seemed that the Lord was calling us to have the heart of our Savior who had compassion on the crowds; crowds of harassed people, crowds of helpless people, crowds for whom He died.

The answer to the need of this great city is not physical or material but spiritual. Those who worship and love the true and living God can in this life enjoy heaven on earth. They have the promises of God. Those who seek first the kingdom of God shall have food and clothes and the basic necessities of life.

Any other relief of the dreadful physical needs can only at best be temporary, as the cause is the spiritual darkness in which the people live. While people worship devils they will live in fear, sloth, dirt, darkness and bondage. The devil will try to bring them even lower than the animals. Those who worship such things, speaking of idols, shall become like unto them.

When the Lord saw the crowds He said to pray to the Lord of the harvest to send forth laborers into the harvest. It is harvest time! Will you pray that we will see such a move of the Spirit that the compassion of our lovely Savior would be in all our hearts so that laborers will go out to bring in the harvest?

We are living in the last days, the days when disease, famine, wars and rumors of wars are commonplace, but praise God, these are also the days when the word of God is available and God is pouring out His Spirit.

Eileen Vincent

CHAPTER 1

WHEN THE SPIRIT CAME

Bombay: 1972

"Where have you been?" Alan's anxious look told me the whole story. I was three hours late. Though only a few miles from home the painful waiting lent plenty of opportunity for imaginations to run wild. I could have been in the hospital or I could have been abducted or any of another thousand horrors!

I was supposed to be home by six o'clock but now it was nine. Exhausted, I sat down and began to tell of wonders and miracles. When the Holy Spirit is poured out ordinary activities soon turn into extraordinary events till every day has the expectation of the extraordinary. I had gone to shop for a few necessary items for the house and should not have been more than an hour, but then I met Frances.

She was grabbing a few last minute essentials for the birthday party. In her excitement she was talking so fast. "Everyone is coming" she said, "Yes aunty from Thana and I've called my friends from work and my grandmother is coming. You know she needs someone to bring her so my cousins will be here too. Oh, I think we will be about forty in the house. What an opportunity! Yes, we're going to tell them about Jesus, yes and we've got music. Ajit is coming with his guitar. We have been praying so much, I know they will all be saved tonight."

Continuing to explain myself I said, "Alan I could not refuse the pressing invitation, I had to go to the birthday party." In those amazing days, any and every opportunity was used to share the gospel in an all-out effort to bring family members, friends and neighbors to Christ. These new

Christians were so overjoyed with their new life that they could not keep quiet. Anyone was a target for their loving witness, even if they had to compel them to listen!

Just trying to walk into the crowded home was like an obstacle course as I was hugged continually being passed from one set of arms to another. The music was already blaring; no one seemed to care about forcing the whole street to listen in. The birthday party was the cover for an impromptu evangelistic outreach. Frances raised her voice and called Leroy to tell what had happened to him. With the same enthusiasm Leroy told his story. He had always gone to Mass and said the rosary, and even went to confession, but now something was different; he had met Jesus. He gave a clear, simple testimony of a revolutionized life now overflowing with joy and love for God. He was evidently filled with the Holy Spirit, his words carried power as he spoke so naturally expecting Jesus to do the same miracles today as He did when on earth. Once he was religious, now he had life. Once he tried to keep rules, now his delight was to obey the Word of God. Stories flowed and questions were asked from all corners of the room. Then demons began to manifest.

"What could I do? Alan, I couldn't get away; I was casting out demons and praying for the sick and many were being led to life in Christ." These new Christians were not satisfied for anyone to accept Christ as Lord and Savior without them obviously being filled with the Holy Spirit. These ordinary new Christians would encourage all the converts to receive the power of the Holy Spirit so that they too would cast out demons, heal the sick and preach the word. The gifts of the Spirit abounded among them. As the revival moved through the Catholic area of Bombay such scenes were repeated many times. These passionate, gregarious people had life, they would not keep quiet; they sang about it, talked about it, and shared Jesus with everyone.

This period of time in Bombay was amazing with wonders as the Holy Spirit was poured out. It was hard to imagine that Frances and her family had been as lost as the guests at the party only a year or so previously. And here I was standing in the middle of a miracle; I would never have thought that the decision we made just nine short years before would bring us to Bombay and revival.

But let me begin at the beginning to help you understand from where we had come.

CHAPTER 2

OUR ROOTS

Alan's parents were from Liverpool, England. The northern influence was always obvious in the family, especially in the food they ate. They had four children and Alan Maurice was the third child born August 19, 1930 in Wimbledon, Surrey, famous for the lawn tennis championships.

The family made their home in Harrow, Middlesex, about fifteen miles outside central London. Alan's childhood years coincided with the terrible days of World War II. Like all families that lived through those challenging times, his parents felt the impact upon their everyday life. Alan's father, a civil engineer, travelled the country with responsibility for repairing the rail bridges and keeping the railways running during the enemy bombing.

His grandmother was converted in the Welsh Revival. The genuine spirituality of this wonderful lady influenced the whole family. Two of her sons went into the Baptist ministry, and to this day, there are those in the family line who serve God in various places of the world. Alan's father, as an engineer, chose a different course for his career.

Alan had the privilege of growing up in a good church-going family where his father served as a deacon in the local Baptist church. Unfortunately the home was not a place where fervent Christian attitudes were expressed or spiritual things discussed. Reading the Bible and praying with their children was never part of their family life. Religion was considered a personal thing, so they did not seek to determine if anyone was truly saved and, it would seem they never asked those searching questions of their children either. One by one the children drifted away into good, respectable, God-fearing, but not God-centered lives. Alan had nothing against the church or God, but that kind of religious life just seemed irrelevant; the attitude of multitudes of materialistic people today.

The whole family tended to be insular, finding it difficult to talk about personal things. Alan's father covered it up by being more extroverted in his ways, always ready with a joke, as well as being a merciless tease to the children. Alan remembers him as a good responsible father, even though he was not overtly affectionate to any of his children and one who could quickly lose his temper over trivial things.

Alan, under duress, suffered through church attendance three times on Sunday. He attended church service morning and evening as well as afternoon Sunday school, without having any memorable spiritual encounter. At school there was a daily half hour Christian assembly but he remained spiritually untouched. Although there were those about him who did live a true Christian witness, it failed to make an impression upon him.

War was declared when Alan was nine years old. Living near to London meant that the family was never far from action. One time when he was cycling to school a V2 rocket landed in the garden of a house nearby. He was blown off his bicycle by the blast. Getting up from the ground, he saw a bus at the bus stop with all its windows blown out and a crowd of people groping their way from the bus with blood streaming down their lacerated faces from the flying glass. Even school children were in daily danger, with death and injury for all to see, but there is no hint that these horrible events pressed Alan to seek the Lord.

I am convinced the Lord preserved Alan's life on that occasion and again on another. It was the day for celebration when at last the war was ended. Everyone in the road was out preparing a street party. Alan, with his friend, was working on the amplification system for the day's events. Something was not working well, so after testing the system they decided to earth the equipment more efficiently. Alan standing on the damp ground grabbed the bare wire to earth it, but someone had turned on the power. Suddenly 240 volts were crashing through Alan's hand. He fell to the ground unconscious. Fortunately, most men were well trained in first aid as they had to always be ready to help any who were war casualties.

With not a moment to lose, Alan was receiving artificial respiration, while the mother of his friend was beside herself thinking her son had killed Alan. He was soon revived with the help of the excellent treatment from the neighbors, though his hand was badly burned. The Lord was watching over Alan; He had plans for him that would be revealed at the right time. The day would come when he would serve Him and do all His will.

Alan gained entrance to the local grammar school; he was a good student with a natural inclination to the sciences. When the time came for him to leave school, the perfect opening was presented with a position in the Kodak research laboratories, which would use his scientific abilities and give him further training. It was an easy decision. He was being offered a golden opportunity when many young people in the post-war days could not go to study for a university degree. He enjoyed life, including playing rugby football; even breaking his nose did not deter him. Later, that break and a number of other such injuries caused him much trouble.

My family background was very different. My father, Edgar Bowden, was born into a large London family in 1908. His twin brother died in infancy. Family and neighbors supported each other when new babies arrived or in times of trouble. Mrs. Milledge, a big-hearted friend and neighbor, willingly offered an extra pair of hands and tiny baby Edgar was passed over the fence so that she could give him the undivided attention he needed. If anyone had any spiritual influence in my father's life, it was Mrs. Milledge, his godmother. When she was dying, my father, who always had affection for her, took me to her home and there on her bed, was a cherished bible. She was always a devout Anglican.

At fourteen years old my father was apprenticed to his own father as a carpenter and joiner. They constructed pianos for a large London furniture company. The family was nominally Church of England, but there is no evidence that anyone served the Lord or even attended a church. My father was a good-looking young man and it did not take long for my mother, Violet Booth, a very attractive young woman, to fall in love with him. They were married in 1931.

My mother's parents were also from London. Her father Alfred Albert Booth served in the Royal Artillery for twenty-one years, with some of that time spent in India. After his discharge from the Army, he married Rose Casey from a London Irish family and then he became a school caretaker. Violet, born in 1912, was one of three children.

There seems to have been some Christian influence from my grandfather's side of the family. When D. L. Moody was in London, twice he took my mother to the crusades. Possibly, it was about this time, that as a young person, she made a confession of faith and was baptized in a local Baptist church. Unfortunately, whatever happened to her then never grew into a mature Christian life so that I have no memory of either parent ever visiting the church or having any spiritual life.

My parents moved out of London into an area of new development in Hoddesdon, in Hertfordshire. There they purchased a new house and established themselves for many years to come. It became home for their four daughters. I was the second born and arrived on October 9, 1934.

Our childhood years were the war years. Living twenty-five miles out of London meant that we did not have to endure the heavy bombing that was the horrific nightly experience of those living in the city. I was only five years old when war was declared, so although the tensions of life must have influenced me, I do not remember being frightened. To the contrary, I recall sitting on the window sill in the bedroom watching the air battles overhead with the curtain wrapped around me so that no light could escape from the room.

There were many occasions when enemy planes would be flying overhead and we would scan the sky for the notorious doodle bugs with their menacing drone wondering where they would fall. The V2 rockets made their presence known by the very loud characteristic whoosh; then we waited for the explosion that erupted only moments later.

Every conceivable thing was rationed, but we never went hungry. As we walked to school every day we picked up shrapnel fallen from the "dog fights" the night before "to help the war effort". If the air raid siren sounded, the whole class would walk in an orderly "crocodile" down into the dugout, the underground air raid shelter, that took up a part of the playground.

My father was drafted into the Royal Air Force in 1943 and was sent to the war in the Far East, where his unit travelled behind the British troop lines repairing aircraft. As he walked off to the station carrying his kit bag over his shoulder, I sat on the red-tiled front door step and cried and cried. My Dad was my friend and now he was gone. I missed him so very much. He used to protect me as my relationship with my mother was never a happy one. I became a sullen withdrawn child and though only eight years old, would spend as much time as I could in my friend's house next door rather than be home.

My mother found life on her own very hard. Father had left almost immediately following the death of another little daughter who had struggled for life. Sadly, this was their second infant bereavement. Home was not a happy place.

Our mother sent all us girls to the Methodist Sunday school on Sunday afternoons. I'm sure that gave her a needed respite from four demanding youngsters, but perhaps she also remembered her own youthful decision and wanted us to have that same opportunity to hear the gospel. I have many treasured memories from those childhood Sunday school days. Kathy Taylor, severely crippled with rheumatoid arthritis and confined to a wheel chair, was my favorite Sunday school teacher. She left the deepest impression upon me. I was only about seven years old, but she made Jesus so real that I never wanted to miss a Sunday.

About this time, a young African pastor came and spoke to the children. We rarely saw any black people, his appearance as well as his stories of missionaries intrigued me so at the end of the meeting I spoke to him. I had been looking at his hair and wanted to feel it so he lifted me onto his lap and I put my hand on his head touching his strange springy hair. That Sunday afternoon God spoke to a little seven year old girl and set the course of my life forever. As I went home with my sister I skipped ahead saying, "I want to be a missionary when I grow up! I want to be a missionary when I grow up!"

During the long summer holidays we children would play in the fields. For me they were a place of wonderful freedom. From my earliest days I was fascinated with nature and all the handiwork of God. When others were playing, I would collect wild flowers and examine everything that grew and I would be so excited if I found a plant I had never seen before. I would be intrigued with insects, the beauty of cobwebs and sight and sounds of the different seasons. Those loves have endured over the years and have been handed on to my children and grandchildren. I remember lying on my back in the garden looking at the wide, blue sky and being filled with the wonder of its vastness. Somehow in my mind God was up there.

Once the fields were cleared and the harvest was reaped, we children would pick up the gleanings, which were choice pickings for the chickens. Prisoners of war from Italy and Germany were the man-power for the farms. They worked in the fields bringing in the grain as most of the able-bodied men had been conscripted into the armed forces.

I shall never forget the day my younger sister got head lice. My mother was beside herself. She shouted, "You must not go near those prisoners", thinking that was where my sister had contracted the head lice. The men missed their families and always talked to the children. Mother was unable to get any treatment for my sister and resorted to dousing her head with kerosene. Many years later I saw the same treatment used in India. My sister's screams terrified me so that I dreaded ever getting head lice. That night in bed with my head under the covers, I talked to God. I asked him to never let me get head lice. There in the dark, the prayer of a little girl was heard as I transacted in faith not even knowing what I was doing. I knew God had heard me and I knew I would never get head lice.

Many years later when I was travelling in Nepal with our youngest son David sitting beside me on a bus going from Kathmandu to Pokhra, that prayer of faith was lifted out of the past into a very pertinent now. Squashed in the back of the bus next to a diminutive Nepali lady, we were being bitten by bugs coming out of the seats as they found in us a good meal. If that was not enough, looking hard at the little lady pressed up against us I saw head lice, lots of them walking in her hair and hopping around! My first instinct was to try to protect David and myself from them, but out of nowhere, the Lord spoke to me. "Eileen, don't you remember?" I was immediately transported from the back of the bus to that holy place under my blankets years before. The transaction of faith by a seven year old still held good many years later in the back of a bus in Nepal. I never got head lice all the years in India though there were always plenty to catch!

Long after my sisters had given up going to church, I would go alone. The adults provided me with relationships that made me feel valuable. I passed through Sunday school winning attendance prizes each year and awards for Scripture examinations. I was always eager to be in the Christmas and Easter productions. The local churches would have an annual Eisteddfod in which we would compete with bible memory verses, recitations, and singing. One year I sang and won a prize. I was so surprised as my sisters could all sing so well, but I never thought I could.

As I came into my teen years I would be in church three times each Sunday, not because I was sent, but because I enjoyed it. My mother would chide me, "Why don't you take your bed and stay there!" They thought my interest very strange. By the age of fifteen I was received into the membership of the church and was considered to be a good little Christian. I thought I was too. I certainly tried hard and began the habit of daily Bible reading and prayer. In a sincere way I was seeking God. I always knew there was a God; it would have posed too many problems for me to think otherwise.

About this time my heart was very tender to spiritual things. The Easter Sunday message impacted me deeply. The Rev. Huett described our Lord Jesus being nailed to the cross for our sins and the Holy Spirit took the words and pounded them into my heart. I cried as he graphically told how the cross was picked up. I recoiled inside as I felt the shuddering thud and the jarring of the Lord's body as the cross was dropped into the hole.

I had passed the entrance examination into the local grammar school, but never realized the full benefit of the good education available to me. I showed no great aptitude in any direction so, when considering my future career, discussion at home always ended up in the same place. "You will have to do a shorthand and typing course and take a nice little office job." I had a built-in reaction against this. It seemed so dull to me.

I wanted to be a nurse, but my father said, "You will end up washing floors. A nurse's life is not what it appears." He was adamant.

Undeterred, I deliberately gathered information about a good nursing course which students could join at seventeen years of age instead of the normal age of eighteen. I wanted to leave home so badly but knew I could never afford to provide for myself. After much thought I concluded a safe place to go was a residential nursing school so I applied. Eventually, a letter came giving me the date for an interview. When the day arrived to go, I put on a brave face to cover my apprehension as I walked out of the house. For the first time I would be traveling alone through London and then onto the hospital in Stanmore. The return journey was so different. I felt triumphant. I had been accepted, I was going to nursing school. I was leaving home.

My sister Maureen was attractive and intelligent, but I was never able to get along with her; somehow, we were always 'at daggers drawn'. She was my mother's favorite and I was jealous. But the day I put the shabby leather case on the bed and wondered what one packed when leaving home, she was there trying to be of help. The black bible I had received as a prize in the Anglican Church after I completed the confirmation class went in with my other belongings and we closed the lid together. As we heaved the case to the floor, I realized it was going to be too heavy to carry the mile to the station. "If I wheel it on my bicycle, would you bring the bike back for me?" I asked. She readily agreed and in that moment I felt fond of her. I knew I was going to miss her and all the family.

As my father tried to say goodbye, he said, "If you go, you will not come back here again." He didn't mean it, but felt very opposed to his daughter living away from home and doing what he considered a poor job. I loved him very dearly and hated to see him upset, but nothing was going to stop me. With the case balanced on the bicycle, we walked the familiar road to the railway station, my mind whirling with mixed emotions. I was going to go even though I was biting back my tears.

Little did I know that I would never return to that house again. Shortly after I left, my parents sold the house and moved to a new town. My childhood life was gone with only one short glance back. I was on my own.

CHAPTER 3

MORE THAN NURSING

It was 1951 when I began my course as a student nurse at the Royal National Orthopedic Hospital in Stanmore, Middlesex. This renowned hospital in the south of England is the home of the Institute of Orthopedics. The first three months of nursing training were spent in school. I had had little interest in school subjects such as history, English and mathematics, but now everything I learned captivated me. I enjoyed anatomy and physiology and all the wide variety of new subjects that were presented. For some reason nothing seemed difficult.

Three months flew by and soon it was time to begin working with actual patients. I was assigned to a children's ward where I was astonished to see little ones in total body casts; others severely paralyzed, tried to heave their weak little bodies around. Still others coped with grotesque deformities. Everything was new, emotionally challenging but full of interest. What could I do when a one year old, with his legs in bulky casts so that he could barely move, called endlessly for Mummy? The polio epidemic had hit the nation about the same time as it did in the USA. So many people were crippled by this cruel disease which knew no boundaries for age or social status. I was seventeen years old living daily with heart-rending situations. I began to grow up fast.

No longer did I have the support of my home church so, I went to find the nearest fellowship and tried to make it my habit to attend whenever I was off duty. In the hospital I joined a christian fellowship group and met other Christians. I continued to read my Bible and tried to be faithful to what I understood of Christ.

Frances, the student nurse in the adjoining room, sat down on my bed. As she made herself comfortable, she said, pointing to the Bible on the table, "Do you read that?"

I was in a time of seriously seeking God and trying to find reality in church and Christianity; so I could truthfully say, "Yes, I am reading it every day". Somehow I knew that within its pages was the answer to my quest.

"Perhaps you would like to come to church with me, said Frances, there are special meetings each evening where the Rev. John Stott is preaching."

I had heard his name before and was eager to find a deeper meaning to my Christianity, so Frances did not have to ask me twice.

The next evening found us seated together at the back of the famous London church, All Souls, Langham Place. I listened with rapt attention. The preaching was compelling and new to me. I felt so drawn that I went again the next evening, this time by myself. At the end of his sermon, John Stott invited those who wanted to receive Jesus as their Savior to come to the front of the church.

I wanted to go forward but I didn't move. I sat there in my seat feeling very disturbed and tried to pray so as to get my emotions under control. All I could do was cry; the preaching had challenged me. I knew the pastor was talking about something I didn't have, but I didn't know what it was and I didn't know how to get it! I was confused as I tried reaching into a realm that I did not understand.

The church was emptying about me but I remained seated. A few earnest people were at the front of the church engaged in conversations with counselors. I looked up to see who it was with such a warm voice asking if she could help me. I learned that she was a South African nursing sister from Queen Charlotte's Hospital. Recognizing my troubled state, she talked to me about Jesus and invited me to return the following evening for a bible class designed to disciple those who responded.

The following evening found me again at the church but somehow I felt I didn't belong; not an uncommon feeling for me. It seemed, whatever the situation, I was always on the outside looking in. Seeing the joyful faces round the small room, I knew they had found this 'something' that continued to elude me. The whispered suggestions in my mind were loud and clear, *"You're all right as you are; you're a good Christian, you always have been."* The voices won; I never went back again. My spiritual disquiet subsided; with it my interest in church going and the desire for Bible reading evaporated. When I look back on that experience, it was as if I had put out my hand to reach for that 'something', but however far I stretched it remained just beyond my grasp. Maybe the Lord allowed my eyes to be closed at that time because He had planned some significant events for my life before I would be able to see.

CHAPTER 4

DANCING INTO DESTINY

Hospital life was fairly cloistered, the occasional dance being a major event in a monotonous calendar. There was an unusual buzz of excitement in the nurses' hostel; notices had been put up announcing a barn dance. "Oh! I must have something new to wear," was heard from many quarters, but quickly followed by the sigh, "But I've no money!"

A picture in a woman's magazine caught my eye. It was just a simple gingham skirt with a scarf and white blouse. I bought some material and with the help of the communal sewing machine, I soon had a skirt just like the one in the magazine. An old school blouse was resurrected and with the scarf across my shoulders, I was ready for the dance. There was always a shortage of men for these occasions, so an open invitation had been given to the men at the nearby Royal Air Force station and local scout leaders. These men assisted in the boys' ward by organizing the severely crippled boys into a handicapped troop.

The band struck up and the eager nurses were claimed by their partners. The evening began. A tall, slim, dark haired man asked me for the first dance. He introduced himself as one of the scout leaders; he didn't smile easily but seemed rather serious and intense. As I took his hand and he led me to the floor, I noticed he had very cold hands and they didn't warm up all evening. However, he danced the barn dances with great gusto and huge concentration, his long legs taking enormous strides, making me run to keep up with him. With energetic zeal we continued till the last dance. Little did I know that in just over a year I would be marrying this tall man and for the rest of my life I would be running to keep up with him.

The following day my friend Angela shouted, "Eileen, Eileen, that man you were dancing with last night is on the phone. He is asking, "Who was the girl wearing the pink skirt and white blouse?" He had forgotten my name, but was very intent in arranging a time to meet together again. When his trusted motorcycle was out of service, he would walk miles to come to see me in my off duty hours. We had fallen in love and wanted nothing else but to be together.

At this point of life, Alan had completed eighteen months compulsory national service in the Air Force and had then returned to work in the research laboratories at the Kodak Company. He was now a valued member of the team. Soon his success resulted in his obtaining patents on certain inventions.

Once discharged from the Air Force, he returned to his friendships in scouting where he helped with the younger boys. Most of his activities were centered in these relationships. Together they camped, hiked and enjoyed the outdoor life. Alan continued to be a member of his old school rugby football club and regularly played during the season, but he was beginning to have some problems. Since breaking his nose, he had experienced repeated nose bleeds that became so profuse that he had to go to the hospital more than once to get the bleeding stopped. Heavy bleeding became an everyday event. Drained of physical energy he eventually found playing rugby football too demanding. He only discovered how serious the problem was when he went to give blood at the local donor station. The nurse sent him away with a bottle of iron tablets and told him that he needed the blood more than they did this time.

In the impetuosity of love we planned our wedding at very short notice. One evening, like so many young lovers, we asked the question, "Is there any reason for us to wait this long to be married? What's stopping us? We could be married in three weeks!" That was how long it took to get a marriage license. In no time at all the decision was made. Our carefully laid plans to be married six months later in the summer were cast aside as together we went into the sitting room to announce to Alan's mother that we planned to be married in three weeks' time! In her usual unemotional manner she listened and told us how she would help.

Christmas was only three weeks away and we were pushing our plans into the family's well-laid Christmas arrangements, quite oblivious to our own selfish behavior.

Soon we were in a whirlwind of organization. Where were we to marry? And what kind of wedding was it to be? Alan was happy for a civil affair, but to be married in church and before God was very important to me. I chose the hymns and readings carefully and prayed fervently for God's blessing on our wedding. We were married in Hendon Methodist church in North London, on December 22, 1953 with a small family gathering in attendance.

Within six months we were fortunate to be able to buy a comfortable family-sized home that left little money for furnishing, but nothing mattered. We had grown up with the shortages of the war years and were quite used to making a little go a long way. We budgeted carefully and slowly furnished room by room, enjoying painting and modernizing our home. The following year we were busy working on a nursery. It looked lovely and we waited with anticipation for the arrival of our own baby. It seemed so amazing that soon we would hold our own child. We tried to imagine how being parents would impact our lives.

CHAPTER 5

THE NEW BABY

I had asked my doctor if I could have our baby in Queen Charlotte's Hospital in London. My request was motivated in part by the memory that the South African nurse who counseled me worked at that hospital.

The pregnant mothers attending the antenatal clinic were invited to tour the hospital to see where their babies were to be born. Imagine my surprise when one part of our tour was conducted by this same South African nursing sister who had talked with me in the London church at John Stott's meeting four years earlier. Of course, she didn't recognize me but I immediately knew her. I hung back behind the other women wondering whether to speak to her, but before there was opportunity, we moved on to the next department.

"Mrs. Vincent, you have a son." I felt so happy. We had so wanted a boy. I took the baby in my arms for a moment and looked at the funny little creased up face. Such emotions flooded over me. *"How amazing this baby is mine"*, I thought. He looked a little blue but I did not think too much of it, after all some babies are blue when just born.

"Thank you, Mrs. Vincent, we will just take the baby and keep him over here for a while." He was whisked away. I relaxed, felt my flattened tummy and went to sleep. When I eventually woke, an efficient nurse was by my side bringing me breakfast. I had been put into a side room alone and for a moment wondered why. I asked the nurse if I could see the baby. "A little later he will be brought to you," she replied and left the room.

I looked up quickly as the door opened. The ward sister walked in followed by a nurse pushing a baby's cot. I realized something was wrong.

The sister quickly spoke, "Mrs. Vincent, your baby is a little blue and we shall have to keep him in this oxygen tent for a time. The pediatrician will see him later today." Then kindly she asked, "Will your husband be coming today? Let him see me when he arrives." Silently, the cot was eased out of the door. The visit was all over. Within one minute the baby had come and gone and the door was shut. I looked at the door and repeated the sister's words to myself again and again. I tried to visualize the baby; yes, he had looked very blue, but in every other way he was a perfect little boy with a good weight.

"Shall we move you into the main ward? You will be much happier there." With those few words, my belongings were gathered together and I was escorted across the corridor to a ten-bed ward.

At last visiting time came. With one look at Alan's face, I could see that he was upset and more than that, I could see he did not know what to say or do. The pediatrician came to see us both. In a very deliberate voice she said our baby had congenital heart disease and was very ill. After a few days the medical team hoped to be able to x-ray him and perhaps perform an emergency operation. She went on to say, "But he will require further surgery when he is stronger." Then she continued, "In such cases, Mr. Vincent, there is only a slim chance of life." I felt the bottom had dropped out of my world. I had no resources within to meet this kind of calamity. The heartless bell rang, signaling the end of visiting time. Friends and family members made their noisy farewells, drifting out in ones and twos, taking a last peep on the way at their new babies, grand-babies or other happy additions to the family. Soon, all was quiet.

"Would you like the baby to be baptized, Mrs. Vincent?"

The question jolted me. *"So they don't expect him to live. What happens to babies when they die?"* I asked myself. Then I heard myself saying, "Yes, please do arrange for him to be baptized."

The ward sister answered, "The Methodist minister will be here tomorrow; he will see to it."

As she walked away from the bed I began thinking about death. It seemed like a vast, frightening unknown. Who thought about death when only twenty-one years old? My mind was racing; *"My baby is going to die—he is going to meet God. What is it like to die? Yes, let him be baptized—if it is going to help."* But somehow I didn't feel convinced. I put my head under the sheet and sobbed. I pleaded with God to help my baby and not to let him die. I visualized the awful wall chart entitled, "The Deformities of Congenital Heart Disease" that used to hang by my desk in the nursing school. "Deformities; heart disease," the words rang in my ears. The grotesque pictures were vivid in my mind and I thought, *"My baby is going to grow up like that."* I cried out to God, "Let him die, let him die, it will be better if he dies." Then I wept and wept, condemned in my heart that I should ever say such a thing.

The seeming endless days ran into one another. With the clatter of the nurse's trolley I was suddenly awake. All the lights were on in the room though outside the grey darkness of early morning still shrouded the view. *"Was our baby still alive?"* I waited anxiously to ask the nurse as soon as she came near. In my confused dreaming that night I had asked that question dozens of times and received many different answers, though now awake it still seemed a nightmare.

"Yes, the baby is well and looks a little pinker today." Hope soared within me. *"Perhaps he will rally sufficiently for the operation,"* I thought. My mind raced on; *"The Methodist minister is coming today to baptize him."* We named our little son Nicholas Alan. I thought, *"Surely I will be able to see little Nicholas today—perhaps even hold him."*

The curtains were drawn round the bed next to me and shortly a priest came to give Holy Communion to the patient. I lay in bed reverently quiet, wistfully thinking of the days when I used to take communion and go to the Methodist church. Within me, there was a longing for something I couldn't really explain. I remembered the time in All Souls, Langham Place and wondered if the South African sister would ever come into my ward. I would have loved to have talked with her.

During afternoon tea time the ward sister visited each patient. Standing by my bed she said, "You will be pleased your son was baptized at two o'clock this afternoon."

"Oh!" I said. "But I so wanted to be there; I thought you would tell me when the minister came as I did want to talk to him myself."

"He came during resting time Mrs. Vincent; it would not have been very advisable to disturb you. Baby is a little pinker today; let's see how he is tomorrow."

As she walked away a cold, heavy feeling settled in my stomach. I had longed to see my baby. Feeding times were an agony as I watched the other mothers with their beautiful new babies. I planned to ask if I could go to the nursery to see Nicholas the next day. Looking back now, I realize the hospital regulations in those years were very onerous, though at the time, I accepted them. Nicholas was in the equivalent of an intensive care unit which allowed no visitors. Alan was taken to a viewing window but it gave little satisfaction.

The following morning, before I had opportunity to make my request, a nurse entered the ward and came straight to me. "I'm sorry, Nicholas is not so well; he nearly died in the night but has rallied now. Yes, you can come to see him; we will call you a little later." As I waited, a war waged back and forth in my mind between painful fears that alarmed me and trying to think hopeful thoughts which really didn't convince. Finally the nurse called and I was escorted along the corridor. All the doors looked alike. The nurse peeped through the glass panel and beckoned me to follow her. I had been given a mask to cover my face, but now it covered my anguish as I looked at Nicholas. Grey blue, gasping in the oxygen tent, he looked practically lifeless. His little hands were so beautiful; the finger nails a perfect shape. Nobody said a word. I walked slowly back to the ward, weighed down with such heavy thoughts and indelible impressions.

"Oh God! Oh God!"; I didn't know what to say. I didn't know what I wanted God to do. I was afraid. I was afraid of having a hopelessly deformed child, incapable of normal life and I was afraid he would die. I sobbed and sobbed; "My baby! Oh Lord, help my baby!"

The nurses bustled around; the babies cried, were cuddled and fed. No one mentioned Nicholas. I assumed he must still be living but I didn't want to ask. Beds were being straightened and everything tidied to military precision as visiting time approached. I had felt somewhat remote from Alan each time he came. He had withdrawn into himself. I couldn't enter into his distress and he couldn't comprehend what I was feeling. Regardless of our lack of verbal support, just his presence was a comfort. I had no need to explain myself to him. The visiting time passed all too quickly but, unknown to me, he would soon be back again.

The ward sister came in and pulled the curtains round my bed. Standing close to me, she said, "I am sorry to tell you, your baby has just died. Will your husband be visiting you now, or shall we phone him?" Alan drew back the curtain and stepped inside. His eyes, full of tears, searched my face. We had no words for each other. Our tears mingled on my cheek as our grief burst in soul-wrenching sobs.

Nicholas had lived for four seemingly endless days. His short life ended on the sixteenth day of February 1955. I had seen many mothers leave the hospital with happy family in attendance, all vying to carry the new baby. Now it was my turn to go. I collected my belongings to the embarrassed looks of the other mothers who could not think what to say. Once home, the beautiful little nursery we had prepared was ready with everything expectant. Now I could not bear to go inside; it seemed cold and dead.

Neither of us knew how to start life over again, so when I suggested attending church the following Sunday, Alan was quite happy to take me. I was seeking a comfort that no one could give me and instinctively felt that it could be found at church; but where to go? We had often noticed a happy crowd of people outside the Baptist church, so we decided to try there. The building was full when we arrived, so we sat near the back by the steward who looked after the door. The service was soon over; nothing had reached the hunger I felt or brought me any comfort. Somehow I was numb. Disappointed, we walked away and never returned there again.

The following months proved to be very difficult. I continued to be upset by the loss of our baby Nicholas. I was advised, "Look, you are so young; why don't you sell your house and move into London, get a new job and have some fun?" That kind of advice seemed so hollow; I knew it wasn't the answer. Somewhere there must be something that can satisfy the deep needs of the heart.

CHAPTER 6

NEW BEGINNINGS

Nottingham, England: 1956

Alan stood with his hands upon his hips and admired the stripes on the lawn. Satisfied, he stretched his tall, lanky body and pushed the mower away. The new garden was gradually taking shape. We weren't experts at gardening and Alan was still learning to distinguish weeds from plants, but already the results of our efforts were a great source of delight to us. We had moved into this lovely bungalow the previous year when Alan took a new appointment as a lecturer in the Nottingham College of Technology.

It had all happened seemingly by chance. Alan, young and ambitious, was frustrated working in the research laboratories of the Kodak Company because promotion seemed so slow. Despite his frustration he had an insatiable love for his work which totally absorbed him. To think he was paid for what he so enjoyed, amazed him. Alan had worked at the Kodak Company since leaving school and, in those few short years, had enjoyed success and promotion. He was part of an excellent team working on the development of chemicals and materials for the film and printing industry.

In the evening when I left the dental practice where I worked, I would drive past the factory hoping that Alan would be ready to come home too. He never seemed to be concerned that it was 5:30 p.m. Office doors banged, as people left for the day and soon he would be alone in the building. The men in the factory, who had watched the clock waiting for the blast of the factory hooter, hurried out of the gates as one man. I would wait for Alan at our prearranged place where I had a good view of the laboratory. Those were days before cell phones so we had developed our own signaling system. If he was preoccupied and did not wish to come home, Alan was to come out onto the fire escape steps which were visible from my parked car. His white coated figure would appear like a strange statue pointing homeward, his signal for me not to wait as he was engrossed in what he was doing. So, I would reluctantly go home alone.

One evening at home I looked over to Alan, the soft light highlighted his face. His deep frown and serious mouth made him appear worried, but I had learned to read his expressions and I knew this to be his 'thinking look'.

"Hey, look at this," Alan said, pushing a technical journal under my nose. I put the iron down and took the magazine to the light.

"A lecturer's post in Nottingham", I read aloud. "But you wouldn't want to live in Nottingham, would you?"

"No, that's not the point," said Alan, running his fingers through his shock of black hair. "I was thinking that if I applied for the post now, then Kodak would feel inclined to give me a maximum pay increase at Christmas. They would want to keep me and I've absolutely no intention of leaving Kodak." But it didn't turn out like that.

To his surprise, in spite of his youth and lack of the right academic qualifications, Alan was offered the senior lecturer's position in the new prestigious College of Advanced Technology. The appointment required him to teach chemistry as it applied to the printing industry. For Alan, this would be easy; it was his area of greatest experience and familiarity.

The discussions became serious. What were we to do? It would be a major upheaval leaving friends and selling our home. Nottingham, though only 130 miles away seemed like another world. Alan considered he was worth more money and he knew it would not be forthcoming in his present position for a year or two and this new post offered nearly twice his present salary. The discussion was short, the decision was easy. We quickly pulled up our roots and moved to Nottingham, a fine city in the Midlands of England. What a change came into our lives! The city had history; the old cobbled streets could tell their own stories. We enjoyed just walking round the town taking in all the new sights and smells. With everything new about us, we set out to enjoy our new home town with more money than we ever dreamed we would have at this young stage in our lives.

When Alan went to arrange a mortgage for our new bungalow, the manager said, "I can see Mr. Vincent that you are a man of substance"; something Alan has never forgotten! We bought a car, the first since our marriage. We were enjoying our new affluence.

Nottingham had a good theater where we occasionally went in the evening. There the social set would meet and those who thought they were somebody in the city would be present and engage in small talk over wine and cheese. It was never quite our scene. Alan was never given to small talk and always far too earnest and shy around new people.

Our bungalow, with its large picture windows and commanding corner site, was for us a symbol of our prosperity and success. We pottered in the garden, weeding and planting; we were content. Saturday afternoon is not the usual time for salesmen to come calling so I couldn't help but notice two young men going from door to door. I assumed they must be selling something as doors seemed to open and shut rather briskly. As they came nearer, I saw that they didn't look very English, and I was all the more curious. With one eye on my weeding and the other on them, I surreptitiously watched their progress up the street. Soon they were walking through our gate and with their first words of greeting, I knew these two young men were American.

Alan left what he was doing and came over to talk. They introduced themselves as missionaries and said, "We have come to your country to spread the truth about the Church of Jesus Christ." This sort of thing didn't interest Alan very much. He had given up church when he was about thirteen in preference for Sunday scouting. As they continued to talk we found the two young visitors very interesting. Perhaps our impression was colored by the desire we had often expressed of emigrating to the United States. We were keen to hear first-hand of life and conditions on the other side of the Atlantic and the young men were ready to talk. Alan had always thought that prospects for his personal advancement were better there.

The conversation turned to a return visit and soon they were inviting themselves to come the next Monday evening. "Will 8 o'clock be convenient?" they asked. "We will explain our teachings from the bible and afterwards we could tell you a little about the States." Before we knew what had happened, we had agreed to their next visit.

The next morning, we got up late as usual. Sunday was always one of those self-indulgent days in which we never knew what to do with ourselves. I loved lying in bed, but then the rest of the day I felt slightly frustrated because I had wasted my time. We spent a leisurely hour or two gardening and were enjoying a cup of tea watching the world go by from the vantage point of our large living room window. A young couple came into view and we watched them walk past the house. Alan said, in a contemplative way, "Probably they are off to the cinema." There was a silence. We were both deep in thought. There was a kind of restraint upon us that was without explanation. We had never gone to the cinema on a Sunday or sought any man-made entertainment. That sounds strange today, but for us, Sunday was a different kind of day; a day in which to enjoy long walks in the countryside, or simple pastimes. It was a day to go to church, but that was something we never did.

Monday evening soon arrived and at eight o'clock sharp, there was a knock at the door. In a businesslike manner, the two American missionaries had come as they said. Our embarrassment at talking about spiritual things was soon banished by their efficient matter-of-fact way of handling the situation. We were soon reading verses from the bible which they explained to us. The lesson was all over in half an hour but we had many questions, so we talked informally for the rest of the evening. Alan contended, "I'm an agnostic, perhaps even an atheist." His was not a thought-out position, but one he espoused because he found it convenient in the cynical, scientific world where he worked. The young missionaries were not deterred in the slightest by these comments.

As the American missionaries got up to leave, we warmly agreed to a return visit the following Monday. We had enjoyed our discussion. I tidied the room and gathered up the cups while Alan thumbed through the literature they had left. We had said we would do some homework, answering the questions on a duplicated sheet and reading bible references. Something new was happening.

CHAPTER 7

TWO NEW CREATIONS

In the following weeks, we found ourselves becoming extremely sensitive to spiritual issues. Unanswered questions churned around in our minds so that we found ourselves asking other people what they thought about Jesus Christ. In the evenings we read the assigned bible verses and talked endlessly together about their meaning.

Our teachers came regularly and began to introduce ideas which seemed quite contrary to those we had been taught in our Sunday school and church-going days. We didn't readily accept what they said, so carefully read the scriptures all around the verses they were quoting. Soon it became apparent that their interpretation was not the obvious one. Alan would research the context and often we ended up thinking that the verses did not prove the line of reasoning the missionaries were trying to make.

There came a point when I didn't want them to visit us anymore; it was difficult to tell them because they were very pleasant people. They introduced us to the Book of Mormon, and suggested certain chapters for reading. Neither of us felt at all drawn to the book as it seemed like a poor imitation of the Bible. When we pointed out that if the Book of Mormon was 'divinely given' in the year 1823, why was it written in the old English language of the 1600's? They had no answers.

Almost three months had passed since the Mormons' first visit and during that time something radical had been happening in us. After months of endlessly examining spiritual issues, a mass of doubts and questions had surfaced in our minds. We knew we had to come to the point where we had to make a decision about the Mormon teaching; it had raised all kinds of problems but it was the Bible we turned to for the answers. I did not want to keep thinking about spiritual things but

I could not get them from my mind. I could hardly sleep and felt very troubled. I read the Bible and Alan and I even tried to pray together. About this time Alan was at home during his long college vacation. He had plenty of time to read and think.

In 1958 the 'Cold war' was very hot with shows of strength coming from the nuclear powers and nuclear weapons being freely tested. The world was in a mess. The future appeared gloomy. The specter of a third world war was looming over us and no one had answers to the chaotic situation. One evening I came in from work to meet an earnest looking Alan who had been reading my Bible for most of the day.

He said, "I wish all I have been reading were true—surely then Jesus would be the answer to the world's desperate state."

"True? Of course it is true," I said self righteously. I was pleased that Alan found the Bible interesting and I enjoyed the thought that perhaps sometimes we could go to church together. I didn't want to be the kind of parent who sent her children to Sunday school but who never took them to church.

At work I found myself asking other people their opinion about the Bible and Christ. We laughed together as we talked about those who even believed in the devil! I said, "It is like believing in fairies at the bottom of your garden!" Each evening Alan and I talked earnestly about the scriptures he had read that day, or our understanding of the church, or what it meant to be a Christian. It seemed to be the only subject that filled our minds. Alan's long vacation from college offered plenty of opportunity for him to spend hours and hours reading the Bible. His study had now ventured far from the set lessons. He was drawn to the Gospel of John and found the person of Jesus fascinating. Alan liked the way Jesus won his arguments with the scribes and Pharisees. Jesus was a man to be admired, but the question demanded an answer; was He really God's son or was He someone around whom a huge number of mythological stories had been woven?

I wondered if Alan was becoming too drawn into religious things that neither of us fully understood. My fears were confirmed that evening when our discussion ended abruptly by Alan saying, "Well, if these things are true they mean everything or nothing. There cannot be a halfway attitude when it is a matter of life or death." Now I was sure he was becoming fanatical. Deliberately I responded, "Religion is alright in moderation, but it is dangerous to let it go too far." I felt frightened and didn't know why—I decided not to talk about the subject again, but couldn't shake off the fear. My concern was that if we became too involved it would ruin our marriage.

The Mormons continued their weekly visits but somehow their teaching was no longer of any great interest to us. The only purpose their visits served was to keep the whole mix of spiritual issues hot in our minds. The discussions continued.

My teenage attempts at being a Christian did not stand up to this scrutiny. I was troubled. At night sleep did not come so easily. As soon as I put my head on the pillow a whirlwind of thoughts took hold of my mind. I tried praying, but realized I didn't know how to pray. In my imagination I conjured up a fatherly figure sitting on a great throne up in heaven. Somehow it was all so unreal. I didn't realize God was speaking to me. My restless mind resisted His voice as I tried every way to suppress the troubling thoughts. I was tired. Alan was having similar difficulties, but I resisted talking to him or sharing the intimate deliberations of my heart. I was afraid—a rare emotion for me—and I really didn't know what I was afraid about.

One evening Tony, an acquaintance who was in the army, unexpectedly came to see us. On the table were the Book of Mormon and the Bible which immediately prompted him to ask, "Why are you reading this?" holding up the Book of Mormon. Alan began to tell him of the happenings of the past three months. Tony leaned forward listening intently. Soon they were deep in animated conversation about spiritual things. I left them to it and went to the kitchen feeling apprehensive. This kind of conversation was only going to fan Alan's interest and where would it all end?

Plans were made to go with Tony to the city of Derby to visit his friend who he said could help us. My behavior became quite irrational.

Although for three weeks I had difficulty in sleeping and had no peace with my mind continually churning over spiritual matters; I didn't want to go. I didn't want help. I tried to persuade myself I was alright.

Thursday came and Tony arrived as arranged bringing Mary, his girlfriend. In her I found a kindred spirit. She didn't want to go to Mr. Penny's home either so together we planned to visit a Chinese restaurant instead. We got into the car and promptly made our plans known, but the men did not agree with us, Alan backed the car down the steep drive and headed for Derby. He was intent on settling this spiritual issue.

We drew up outside an unpretentious house. It was hard to imagine this was our first meeting with Mr. Penny as he so warmly welcomed us. He introduced himself as Gordon, immediately dispelling any formality. We all sat comfortably as he reached for his well-worn Bible and began answering Alan's questions. As he spoke, I felt disturbed. Soon my eyes were filled with tears. It seemed that what he was saying went right into my heart and made me cry. I tried not to listen; I felt foolish sitting there wiping my eyes with a sodden handkerchief. Pulling myself together I gazed around the room. The piano top was a show place for all the family photographs. Studying each one intently, I tried to work out the various relationships so as to distract my mind from the conversation in the room. But, turmoil raged in my heart with Mr. Penny's words striking home like arrows hitting the mark.

Alan explained that he thought he understood the steps to knowing God but didn't know how to actually meet him, or if such a thing were even possible. He felt as if he had come so far but now there was an impassable river to cross. Gordon helped Alan to understand that it is sin that separates us from God and the only way to be free is to repent. He then showed Alan how Jesus had borne all our sins in His body on the cross and how He died and rose again so that we could be forgiven and receive His eternal life. Questions were answered and there seemed nothing more to say.

"Would you like to receive Jesus as your Savior right now?" Gordon asked. Alan was a very shy person and easily embarrassed about personal things and certainly praying would be considered a very embarrassing thing to do. To my amazement, Alan knelt down with Gordon and prayed. For him, this was the end of questionings and doubts; Alan committed himself completely to Jesus. Gordon's explanations had brought him to a place of understanding and now the gap between understanding and experience was bridged. As Alan reached out in faith and received Jesus as his Savior, suddenly doubts were gone; no longer did he wonder if God was knowable now he had genuine experience. Confidently he could say, "I've met the Lord!"

He got up from his knees and just stood there. No one spoke. Standing before me was a different man; a new man. We had been married four and a half years. I could recognize Alan's every expression, but now, as I looked at him, I didn't know him. It unnerved me—I stood up ready to leave—I wanted to get out of the house as soon as possible. My deepest fears were being confirmed; this 'religion business' was going to ruin our lives!

Gordon very kindly gave me a handkerchief to help my embarrassed state and then said, "What about you?"

My defenses were up, so I replied, "I have always believed in Jesus; I know He is the Son of God and that He died on the cross to save us from our sins. I used to read my Bible regularly. I know it is the word of God. What else is there?"

Opening his Bible at John's Gospel chapter one, he read one verse to me, "But to all who received Him, who believed in His Name, He gave power to become the children of God."

"Eileen, I know you believe in Jesus but have you ever received Jesus?"

I was compelled to admit, "I don't know what you mean."

Carefully, he explained to me that knowing about Jesus and believing in Him just as a fact of history is not what the Bible means when it talks about believing. Gordon explained I must cast myself totally upon Jesus, like a drowning man grabs help. As a demonstration, he took his Bible and offered it to me and said, "Now imagine this is a gift. When does it become yours?

"I suppose when I take it."

"Exactly, and that's how Jesus becomes yours. He gave Himself personally for you when He died on the cross, but it doesn't do you much good until you receive Him. You will know Him when you reach out and take Him."

I was listening intently but I couldn't look at Mr. Penny's face. Everything he said cut into my heart. Guilty tears continued to roll down my cheeks.

Mr. Penny continued, "But as you can imagine, there are conditions to all this. When you open up your heart and receive Jesus you are welcoming The King of Kings. Submit to Him Eileen; give Him the throne of your life. He will give you peace. Eileen, you have a decision to make. Who is going to run your life? Are you going to remain in charge or will you let Jesus be king?"

He came right to the crux of my problem. I wanted to be in charge of my life. Yes I had a decision to make.

"Would you like to receive Jesus now? Come, let us pray."

Before I knew what had happened, I was on my knees by a wooden chair. A war was raging in my mind, *"Get up, get out of here, this is going to ruin your lives, get out, run!"* Fear had a final onslaught, hurling a host of negative thoughts into my mind sending it into a whirl; but the Lord was there to deliver. I heard myself praying the simplest prayer, "Lord Jesus, come into my heart," and deep down within I was saying *"Lord, I give in, Lord, I give in. I can't fight any longer."* And Jesus came. Peace settled upon me such as I had never experienced before. July 3, 1958, was the turning point of our lives. That Thursday evening we left Mr. Penny's house as two entirely new people ready to live entirely new lives. As we stood saying goodbye, I was bursting with joy. The street lights silhouetted the roofs of the houses opposite; it sounds extreme, but all I wanted to do was to stand on top of the roofs and shout, so that everyone could hear, "Jesus has saved me!"

The following day at work I was telling everyone what had happened. I could not imagine why anyone would not believe! The joy in my heart continued to overflow, to such an extent that the person I saw in the mirror was truly new. My appearance physically changed. A new boldness and confidence was mine so that I wouldn't stop talking about Jesus. We were soon introduced to a church and thoroughly enjoyed being there the following Sunday. As we told of our conversion, the people rejoiced with us.

Monday came and with it the regular visit from the Mormon missionaries. As soon as they stepped inside the door we told them our wonderful news, "We have received Jesus as our Savior."

Their reaction was so different from those at church. "You fools, they said, you have been sold that doctrine of salvation."

In that moment, we knew they were not of the Truth. The more experienced missionary then started angrily quoting one scripture after another. For about two hours he argued, trying to convince us that we were wrong. Returning the following Monday, again they attacked our simple faith. We had no answer for them, but we knew we had Jesus. When I felt my faith being battered, I left the room. Alan stayed, contending with them till it was obvious that they would not be persuaded by the Truth. Then he told them not to return. That was the last of the Mormons. We were thankful that we had resisted all the invitations to attend their meetings. Then we gave thanks to Jesus that, even while we were being taught error, He stepped in and showed us the Truth.

CHAPTER 8

YES LORD! ANYWHERE!

The Call to Missions

Calling out to Alan I said, "Why did you turn the record off?"

"Somehow I didn't like it today; come and listen, see what you think."

I went into the lounge where Alan began to play the record again. He was right. Something within me also felt uneasy listening to those words. "No, that's not for us now."

How our taste had changed; that particular record used to be a favorite. All at once I realized how transformed we were. We no longer went where we wanted, did what we wanted, or listened to what we wanted; we were submitting to what Jesus wanted. Strangely though, His choice was also our choice and we were so happy.

Every area of life had come under a new regime. We had decided that we were not going to follow anyone's rules but we would do everything that Jesus said. So smoking went when Christ came in, the half-finished packet of cigarettes was thrown out. Although Alan never drank more than the occasional glass of wine or beer, the Lord showed him that even that had to go. Each time he refused a drink on some business or social occasion, it made opportunities to tell people about Jesus. In fact, telling people about Jesus became our normal lifestyle. We were always looking for opportunities or, we made them!

Within one week of the glorious day of our new beginning, we were standing on a platform giving our testimonies to a large crowd of young people. I remember being thankful for the short red curtain that hid my trembling knees. But regardless, I was ready to do it again and again. It felt so natural telling people what God had done for me.

We did not need to be persuaded about baptism; for us it was the obvious next step in our Christian lives. We joined the instruction class which met in the home of Mr. and Mrs. Elliott, an excellent deacon and his wife. Little did we know what a privilege was ours, sitting under the tutelage of this wonderful, mature couple. Those Monday evenings spent at their simple home by the railway viaduct were such a joy. There we learned childlike trust and obedience to the word of God. Mr. Elliott was a very well-read plumber. He introduced us to many great missionaries through the biographies he loaned to us from his extensive library. Week by week there would be something new to challenge us. Besides in-depth Bible studies, with a strong emphasis on holiness, we read the biographies of various missionaries. We were confronted by the sacrificial living of C.T. Studd, the faith of Hudson Taylor or the selfless compassion of Amy Carmichael and many others. A solid faith was being established in our lives so that we could declare, "The God of Studd and Hudson Taylor is our God!" The six short weeks of the baptismal class proved to be an excellent training school where we grew, putting our roots down deeply into Christ, absorbing all He gave.

The following weekend presented an opportunity to put some of what we had learned into practice. I could hear my friend Ruth's urgent voice over the phone; she seemed desperate for spiritual help.

Alan looked at me enquiring, "Do they want to come?"

I nodded, and he motioned, let them come. "Yes you are very welcome, just come." For the next hour, we quickly prepared the bedrooms and planned ways to introduce them to Christ so that by the time Ruth and her boyfriend arrived, we had it all planned. We would give them a good meal and then take them to the monthly Youth for Christ rally where we were quite sure they would be converted.

When Ruth and Chris arrived, Alan began talking to Ruth while Chris followed me into the kitchen. He was so eager and concerned that I found myself leading him to Christ as I was trying to fry the fish! We went into the lounge to share the happy news and there found a tearful but joyful Ruth. Alan had explained the gospel and Ruth had been as eager as Chris to receive Jesus. We stood there together praising the Lord! Ruth's mother had become a Christian and had been praying for them; unknown to us we were reaping where she had sown.

We kept to our plan and the four of us went to the Youth for Christ rally. Together we raised our voices and sang lustily, "Blessed assurance Jesus is mine." We were bursting with joy at the wonderful and amazing way God had worked for our friends. It seemed that the whole day had been especially planned just for them.

When we arrived at the meeting, we were surprised when it was announced that the advertised preacher was unable to come and a missionary on furlough was to speak in his place. As soon as he began to preach the atmosphere was charged and his every word gripped our attention. Now it seemed the meeting was not for Ruth and Chris but uniquely for us; every word was ostensibly aimed in our direction. This man had something to say; he was fired with a burning zeal for the lost. His words shook self-centered, complacent Christians. His voice rung out, "It is good to sing, 'Jesus is mine,' but that is only the beginning; get ready for a sacrificial life and be obedient to the call of God."

In his closing words, the preacher lifted a passionate voice as he invited to the front of the church all who would obey a missionary call to go wherever the Lord would send them. The invitation was a simple call to obedience and everyone should have responded. We sang the hymn, "Take my life and let it be, consecrated Lord to Thee". I had sung that hymn dozens of times as a child and then as a young person with the deepest sincerity wishing that every word of it would be true of me. Standing before God that evening, the Holy Spirit found me. I was struggling, feeling I should respond but inside not all was surrendered. Inwardly debating I thought, *"Do You really want me to respond to this call? Are You calling me to go forward? Surely You don't want me to be a missionary?"* Then questions welled up, *"Perhaps it is true; this has always been my calling, but Lord, are You really calling me?"*

Both Alan and I stood in our places not making any attempt to move. Alan was having a similar battle in his mind. For me, this was all very surprising as I thought I was fully surrendered to the Lord. One young man stood alone before the preacher. I admired him, but assured myself the missionary call wasn't for me. The meeting ended and we made our way out. We had entered the hall with such joy, but now left in heaviness.

Once in the car on our way home, I asked Alan what he thought. "Did you get the impression that you should have gone to the front—should we have responded to that call?"

Alan told me that he had been going through the same painful conversations in his head and added, "I felt most uncomfortable. I think God was calling me, but I'm not sure."

I added, "I think God was calling me, but like you, I didn't want to go. The invitation he gave was very broad; would you go anywhere the Lord sends you? I suppose every Christian should say yes to that."

In our prayers together that evening we told the Lord we were sorry for not immediately obeying. "Yes Lord, you were calling us, but we didn't want to hear. Oh Lord, give us a second chance and we'll be first at the front." *Hadn't I said many years before, I'm going to be a missionary when I grow up?*

That second chance came sooner than we had expected with our church's Annual Missionary Convention. The first speaker was a doctor from a tribal area in North India. Alan spoke to him afterwards and told him how we sensed that God was calling us into missionary service. He spoke kindly to us with lots of good advice. He suggested that since we had only known the Lord for about two months, the best thing we could do was to forget about it for the time being and concentrate on growing in the Lord. Glyn Morris, the pastor at the church, also spoke to us in the same manner saying, "If the desire for missionary service doesn't go away, it is probably from God." We felt disappointed. We had said, yes Lord, we'll go anywhere, but now we were being discouraged by the very people we thought would encourage us. We were tempted to think that perhaps our feelings were just emotion.

Despite the seeming discouragement, the Lord confirmed His call in an unconscious way. Over a period of time, we came to an inward knowing that the missionary life was His will for us, but first we needed to mature in Christ and rest confidently that He would locate us to exactly where He wanted in His own appointed time. During the following days we experienced a settled peace. While we waited for our opportunity to go anywhere the Lord would choose, He showed us that we had the power to send others, and gladly we gave ten percent of our income to missions.

Our baptism was a momentous event; as I came up from the water I could have burst with joy. Looking back at that time, had I understood that I could receive the baptism of Holy Spirit as in the Acts of the Apostles, I'm sure my joy would have flowed out in tongues!

To add to the occasion, my sister was also baptized, having come to Christ when she stayed with us soon after our conversion. It happened so simply.

We met her from the train and immediately she exclaimed, "Eileen what has happened to you, you look so different!"

I said, "Wait till we get home and I will tell you all about it." We had only known the Lord for just over a week but she could not fail to see our joy and enthusiasm; she knew something momentous had happened to us both. I did not know how to lead someone to Jesus so I took a small booklet, "The Way of Salvation" and read it page by page, only turning the page when I was sure she agreed and understood. In my zeal to see my sister saved, I was not going to let her go to bed till she had made a commitment to the Lord! We got to the final page and the prayer of commitment; she prayed the prayer and the glorious transaction was done. It seemed so easy—I was ready to do it again!

Very soon we were to leave Nottingham and the church that we had come to love. We had been enriched by the excellent teaching and the warmth of the great fellowship. How little we understood the value of this special place with its powerful mentors that shaped and formed our early days in Christ. Only years later we would marvel at the Lord's grace to us; indelible lessons had been written on our hearts.

Alan left his lecturing position and now, just nine short months after receiving Christ, our possessions were packed into the moving van and we traveled south. Alan was to return to the Kodak research laboratories. We had completed the purchase on the perfect property; but there was one huge dilemma, we had not sold our house in Nottingham. I stayed in Nottingham to assist in selling the house while Alan planned to travel home for the weekends. He was excited to take up his new position and be back in the work environment he enjoyed.

It all sounded so reasonable, but soon we found there was not enough money for two mortgages and all the travel. These uncomfortable circumstances forced us into our first little trial of faith. If we didn't tithe to missions then we could make it! The dilemma dangled before us but the decision was soon made; we would not renege on our promise to give. If Alan couldn't travel each weekend we would trust God and tolerate the separation till the house sold. Almost as soon as the decision was made the Lord gave a supernatural answer. The local Printing College called Kodak asking, "Can Alan Vincent be released during working hours to fill an urgent need for a part-time lecturer two afternoons a week?" The Kodak management immediately agreed and released Alan; they wanted to foster a good relationship with the college. Without our even asking, the Lord provided with this extra money enough for all our extra expenses.

We made our home in Kings Langley, a village in Hertfordshire, twenty-five miles northwest of London. Wandering out of the back garden gate through the fields, picking blackberries in the hedges, being enchanted with the tracery of frost on cobwebs; eating wheat from freshly picked ears, walking nervously through herds of Friesian cows as they stood still and stared, I was back in the Hertfordshire countryside which was home, where I had grown up. I loved it!

The view from our front gate was an attractive hill, with fine houses and well-kept gardens. Early in the morning the gates would click behind men hurrying down the road to the station, off to the 'city'; some with bowler hats, but all with briefcases in one hand and umbrellas in the other. Like clockwork, five days a week, the commuters went and came. For an hour each morning, our little railway station bustled with activity then dozed till the returning evening crowd jolted it back to life.

We joined the local Baptist church in which both halves of the community were represented—the men from the city and the Hertfordshire locals. Before long Alan was leading the young peoples' work and we both taught the children in the Sunday school. On Monday evenings an enthusiastic group of students met in our home; the fruit of Alan's witness at the local college where he taught. Soon they were turning to Christ and the group grew. But what were we to teach these brand new believers? Having this responsibility, when we ourselves were only a year old in the Lord, forced us to seek God and in the process we found ourselves in His Bible school.

A book of topical Bible studies called "Every Man a Bible Student" by Dr. Joe Church came into our hands. The studies were written in the fire of the revival which had spread through Rwanda and the surrounding countries of Central Africa since 1932. Each week we would take it in turns to teach the group. For our preparation we would first teach the lesson to each other. Little did we understand at that time that the Lord had led us to excellent material. It carried the breath of revival which captured our own hearts and birthed a life-long passion of praying for revival. Monday evening became our own Bible school with the Holy Spirit. As we taught the eager students, our own hungry hearts grasped a greater understanding of the principle doctrines of the church. The lessons provided a sound foundation for our own very new faith.

Alan, now back in the research laboratories of Kodak, contented himself with slow promotion in exchange for work which he found absorbing. Full time lecturing had not held sufficient challenge; Alan thrived on solving the problems that the research life presented.

His colleagues were astonished at the change that had come over him during his absence. Instead of belonging to the company rugby football club, now he helped to organize the Workers Christian Fellowship.

Alan was known to stand on the table in the dining room and preach to the factory workers during lunch time. He got into hot debate with the members of the research team on the subject of Christianity and its relevance to every day life. There were those who derided him and others who were drawn. During this phase of life, Alan had a lot of favor with the management and did some excellent work which brought him fast promotion.

Soon we were settled very comfortably into our new life and new home. We satisfied ourselves helping with the youth at church and involving ourselves in local evangelistic ministries but, our Monday evening meetings became the highlight of the week. Filled with joy at seeing the lives of young men and women changed, the thought of leaving and going overseas as missionaries hardly entered our minds.

At the same time, a growing cloud spread over our lives. Alan began to experience serious health problems; not that he was of a mind to give them more attention than absolutely necessary. He was having profuse nose bleeds to the extent that he needed to have blood transfusions. The situation became so desperate that he was bleeding in his sleep, when driving the car, or eating his food or preaching! Hardly a day would pass without some serious loss of blood. The problem demanded that we both become very proficient at staunching the flow. There were times when the blood loss was so much that he fainted. There did not seem to be any medical solution. He became so weak that he found it hard even to digest his food; slowly his extreme weight loss became obvious. Visits to the hospital became more numerous and on many occasions, he was admitted as attempts were made to help him. Nothing was of any lasting success.

With this potentially life threatening situation, it was natural to settle down in Kings Langley and enjoy what we could of a very pleasant and prosperous life. As far as we could see, this was life. When Rachel our precious daughter was born just over a year later in 1960, for a time life seemed complete. We even added a much loved dog to the family. God's calling to overseas missions grew unreal and faded into the past like some extravagant enthusiasm. Spiritually we became dry and as time progressed, very restless.

CHAPTER 9

A SECOND CHANCE

One day on my knees tidying the bottom shelf of the bookcase I pulled out an old magazine. My attention was captured by a half page advertisement for a book. In large red letters it said, "Preparing to be a Missionary". The Lord whispered in my heart, "Send for that book!" and without delay I obeyed.

That evening I told Alan what had happened and this led naturally into a discussion about our spiritual state and our present attitude to God's calling. We realized that doubts had crept in, but worse than that we had to admit that all we really wanted was to remain in our present contented life. We did not want to go anywhere; after all, now we had a baby, a lovely home in a great neighborhood and Alan was very satisfied in his career. Life was wonderful and to top it all, we lived in a beautiful place with every amenity and yes; Alan did have a medical problem that would probably prohibit his acceptance by any mission society.

The book arrived and prayerfully we began reading, expecting God to speak to us. Carefully we studied one chapter each evening, then prayed and wrote down what we felt were the clear directives. This went on for some nights until we reached the chapter headed "Ready to Go" then somehow the book was left in the bookcase and the carefully prepared notes were all forgotten. The blessing of those evenings spent seeking God soon evaporated and again spiritual dryness invaded our lives. After a painful interval of many months we recognized the cause of our unhappy state and repented, took the book out of the bookcase again and sought the Lord. We continued writing notes so that we would have an accurate journal of all the Lord had said during our search. The next step in our quest was to do a Bible study on the missionary call. A new determination had entered into our need to know God's will for our future. When all was done we were so happy as we read though our notes, confident that the call upon our lives was real. We were now so sure, it was easy to be willing and obedient. A new depth of faith had filled our hearts, the call was genuine; we were going to be missionaries.

Wanting one more word of confirmation, we asked the Lord to specifically speak to us in the Sunday morning service at church. We thought we had asked a hard thing, because it was Mother's Day; certainly not a time for a missionary message. The preaching that morning centered upon Naomi and Ruth. Then in quite a dramatic manner Mr. Little, the minister, put his notes aside and preached about the missionary call. Raising his voice and seeming to point directly at us he said, "Why won't you be a missionary?" It was as if God were speaking directly out of heaven! We were shocked. We needed nothing more.

When we had asked the Lord for a final word of confirmation, we had also promised that when it came, we would apply to the Baptist Missionary Society. Without any delay that night we wrote offering ourselves for missionary service with no reservations; we would go anywhere there was a need. We felt an urgency, but the Missionary Society obviously did not! We waited impatiently for their reply. Finally a date was arranged for us to meet the Secretary for Asia to learn something of the work and to discuss opportunities in India.

Though we did not recognize it at the time, our obedience to the Lord and our faith in the validity of our calling was being tested through the confusing circumstances, delays and disappointments. Every call must be tested. We were in the Lord's crucible. Although our contact with the Baptist Missionary Society seemed to be fruitless, God used it to test us in three areas of life.

The first test came in a letter from the Baptist Missionary Society Press in India. Alan was highly qualified and capable in his own field of expertise, but the Press had no use for his qualifications. If he was prepared to learn and do a simple manual job, then they would find a place for him. God gave grace to Alan so that it didn't take him long to accept that nothing was too menial for him, if it was the Lord's calling. Between the random contacts, long delays continued. Finally when it seemed that the press in

India was not interested in Alan, the secretary of the mission suggested that we should consider going to The Congo, Central Africa instead.

The very location of our calling was the next challenge we faced. By this time we felt strongly that we were called to serve the Lord in India, but now even that location was in the crucible of testing. We were brought to the place where we could say from our hearts, "Oh Lord, You know! Take us anywhere, we will do anything."

Finally, our ability to truly trust the Lord for the protection of our family came under the Lord's scrutiny. News stories of massacres, murders and horrific martyrdom of missionaries, had filled missionary magazines. Devil inspired ethnic violence that swept the Congo had erupted into open warfare, forcing missionary families to flee. The Baptist Missionary Society was planning to return missionaries to the field as soon as possible and asked if we would go and be part of the reconstruction of the work. We prayed, "What are we to do?" Now that we had a little daughter, it seemed even more necessary to know if the Lord could protect us. After prayer the Lord gave us peace and we felt that physical danger could not be a reason for us to say "No". If the Lord was inviting us into danger, He would also be our shield and protector. So finding courage, we prayed, "Yes Lord, we will go even if it is into danger; we will trust You." Strangely we never heard anything more from the Baptist Missionary Society, but the Lord had heard our unconditional offer and was sovereignly working out His plan for us. Gradually India loomed large again in our vision; yes, surely that was where the Lord would finally take us.

The various perplexing situations that we passed through all taught their different lessons. None of God's dealings in our lives were futile, although at the time, the lack of clear guidance seemed very discouraging and unsettling. It must have appeared to those who were aware of the confusing circumstances, that we had a problem; we should just settle down and get on with life!

Any situation can produce at least two reactions. Either we can submit to the Lord, believing that He definitely controls our lives and has a purpose in what He is doing, even when we do not understand; or we follow our own best wisdom and end up frustrated and out of fellowship with God.

Alan was given information about a technical teacher's post in a printing college in north India. He asked himself, "Is this the door into the land?" On good advice he applied to the college and received an enthusiastic reply from the Principal of the school, inviting him to come. We carefully read the terms and conditions of employment and the salary scale. We felt enthusiastic about the opportunity. We consulted the missionary who had first advised us of the position, but he said we would not be able to live on the money offered and certainly we should not go! Again we came to a dead end; yet another futile attempt. The invitation from the college was so open and warm that we found it hard to accept the missionary's advice and wondered if we were right to turn it down, just because of insufficient money. God could miraculously provide. Were we to step out and trust Him for this? The Lord never gave us a clear word. We found that difficult when it concerned such an important decision. We waited a long time hoping the Lord would speak to us, till at last Alan wrote saying he would not come.

We acted purely on the advice we had received and without any conviction that God had spoken. We were discouraged, another door was closed and this time we had closed it. The enemy told us we had failed. Unfortunately we hadn't recognized our loving Heavenly Father's gentle teaching in this perplexing situation; He wanted us to humble ourselves sufficiently to receive and value good advice from another.

Again everything went quiet. It seemed not to matter to anyone or to the Lord whether we went to India or not. It could have been so easy to push aside all the words from the Lord and just get on with life again which promised to be so good with far more than we had ever expected. Puzzled and needing to hear a fresh word the unexpected happened. "Would you be happy to provide hospitality to Mr. Roy Hession? He will be here for ministry this weekend." Little did we understand what an amazing blessing and answer to prayer his short visit would be. Before long we were telling him of our great dilemma; were we called to missions or had the Lord shut the door, or worst of all had we shut the door?

We learned that he had been in East Africa with Dr. Joe Church and knew intimately of the revival there. Mr. Hession introduced us to his book, "The Calvary Road", which I read over and over again. As we talked he encouraged us and promised that he would put us in touch with the Bible and Medical Missionary Fellowship (BMMF). He was sure they could help us.

Through this introduction we met some very experienced missionaries. Their help and advice was invaluable. Through their auspices we heard about the need in the Gospel Literature Service Press in Bombay, India. Strangely this brought peace into our hearts concerning the declined invitation. Was Bombay the place where we should go? But there were still many hidden parts of our lives that would come under the close scrutiny of the Holy Spirit before we were ready to go.

CHAPTER 10

LESSONS IN THE MEN'S WARD

Rachel was eight months old and such a beautiful child. I bundled her into her carrycot and put her into the back of the car. My mother-in-law sounded alarmed on the telephone. "Alan seems to be in terrible pain and can't breathe. I think you had better come quickly." Only one week had elapsed since Alan had been discharged from a London hospital where he had been receiving treatments for his nose bleeding. I threw a few things together and headed for his parents' home, wondering all the way what could be the trouble. When I arrived Alan was gasping for breath; he was very ill. That afternoon he was again admitted to hospital, this time with a collapsed lung and the functioning lung restricted by an asthma attack. We were in the Lord's school of faith and there remained many lessons to learn. That first night in the hospital sleep seemed impossible. Between gasps Alan asked, "Why? Why Lord?" But God had not made any mistakes.

The hospital was an old army building still in use since the war years. The wards were open with long rows of beds down either side. Nothing was very private. During the night a drunken man was carried into the ward, his blasphemous shouting and filthy language disturbed all the patients. A few hours later he died still cursing and swearing. As the sudden silence fell upon the ward, Alan cried out in his heart, *"It's too late, it's too late he has gone to hell."* The awfulness of people going to hell pounded upon Alan's mind and heart. The horror of hearing a man enter eternity without Christ in such a rebellious state filled Alan with anguish and grief. A new compulsion came on him; if God would heal him, he had to warn men and women to turn to Christ while there was time.

The doctors considered Alan to be a sickly person and started many investigations including testing him for tuberculosis because he was so thin and under nourished. There was no suggestion that he would soon be released. Alan's condition slowly improved and a few days later he was moved further down the long ward. This was an encouraging sign, as the very ill patients were kept near to the door, handy for the mortuary! Those who improved were moved by slow degrees towards the television set.

There is a dull uniformity about pajama clad people in hospital beds. Social status and intellect cannot be determined at a casual glance, but visiting time brings revelation. Our curiosity was aroused by the loving family who visited the crippled man in the bed next to Alan. He was about forty years old. Alan told me he was a successful businessman who tragically, at the height of his career, had contracted polio that left him bedridden.

Just before Alan had been admitted to the hospital he had had a real breakthrough in his research project that received recognition from the senior staff in the laboratory. His work absorbed him and he loved to feel that he was having success and even better if others acknowledged it. Alan was in that specific hospital bed next to that crippled man for God's purpose and the Lord used the painful situation to speak to Alan. "Look at this man at the height of his success and in the prime of life; his health has gone at a stroke, his success has vanished like a mist." Just one minute polio virus was enough to ruin a whole life. Alan, still very far from well and struggling to breathe saw his own absolute frailty and understood in a powerful new way that he was absolutely dependent upon the mercy of God, even for his next breath. Speaking into the depths of Alan's spirit, in ways that only the Lord could, every area of Alan's self-sufficiency and natural ability was coming under the scrutiny of the Holy Spirit. The Lord intended to bring all things under His Kingship.

His hospital experience became his training school. He was sobered by the lessons he was learning, but the Lord had not finished with him yet; another move and another scenario was planned. As the nurse wheeled his bed further up the ward, she brought it to rest near a man who had been an executive of a large company. Now he was suffering from a chronic chest condition which had made him an invalid so that he was unable to continue to work. His career also had been cut off at the prime of life. Again, Alan was brought to the stark reality; that could be me.

Chatting with his new pyjamaed acquaintance, Alan's mind wandered; he was confronted with his own physical state and wondered what the future held. They were not happy thoughts. Then musing on the good things, he said to himself, *"Kodak has been good to me, there is security working for such a company."* He had regular hours, a five day week in an established organization, plus good insurance and mortgage protection. Added all together, it created a comfortable, impregnable status where everything was provided leaving no need to trust God. He slowly came to recognize how self-dependent he was. The Lord's training program was beginning to have effect. He knew there was no company or organization on earth that could give surety against ill health. Step by step the Lord was showing Alan that true security is only in Him.

Alan's attention was riveted on the page where he read and re-read, "March 29th". The Lord said to him, "You will be discharged from the hospital on March 29th." It took a moment for the words to register. *"March 29th, why that's Friday only four days away."* Alan mused to himself, *"I've not even put one foot out of bed as yet!"* and there was still a long way to go to the television set!

I left baby Rachel with friends and hoped she would sleep; then hurried off to the hospital for visiting time. Alan was waiting to tell me his good news. "You will never guess what has happened today, the Lord has told me I'm going home on March 29th." I looked at his frail body supported on the pillows. He still had great difficulty breathing and for the moment, I had great difficulty in believing.

"Friday—that's in four days' time. You will be home for Easter. That will be lovely.

When does your Doctor come? You will need a miracle to persuade him to let you go", I said.

That evening I asked the Lord to personally assure me about Alan's discharge. In ways that only God can, He utterly convinced me, so that I knew Alan would be home on the twenty ninth, regardless of how impossible it all seemed.

I told my neighbor, Alan would be home Friday. Stepping out in faith, Alan told the man in the bed next to him, "I'll be going home on Friday". There was nothing the hospital staff said to encourage him and even Alan's physical condition did not warrant his discharge. When faith grows to the place where you have absolute assurance that God will do what He says, you do not mind who you tell and the very telling strengthens your faith. Reluctance to speak out and testify is indicative of an unbelieving or wavering heart.

As a further declaration of our faith, I took Alan's clothes to the hospital ready for his discharge. The doctor was not due to see him until the morning of the twenty-ninth. Alan was still completely confined to bed and no one had said anything to him that would even suggest the possibility of him being discharged.

Slowly, the group of doctors and advisors proceeded up the ward discussing various patients' cases. Soon they were gathered about Alan's bed. The physician in charge scrutinized the x-rays and banged Alan's ribs in a musical fashion. Alan had decided not to ask the doctor to discharge him but trusted that he would be made to do God's will. Alan lay there waiting for his comments as the doctor thumbed through his notes. There was a long silence. Then looking up the doctor said, "You have been in the hospital for some time haven't you? What sort of wife do you have?"

"Oh! Very nice" said Alan.

"That may be, but could she take care of you if I sent you home?"

"She was a nurse, I'm sure I would be very well cared for," said Alan.

The doctor didn't know he was fulfilling God's will as he turned to the sister and said, "I think we could let him go home as long as he continues to have bed rest." They moved on to the next patient. Later the ward sister in a teasing manner said, "I don't think you can go home straight away, perhaps in a few days." Alan was left in suspense, he knew what God had said, but how God would do it, he didn't know.

When I arrived Alan was still in bed but before long we were rejoicing. The discharge was granted, he quickly dressed and we were on our way home. We had heard the voice of God, we had believed and had seen the most unlikely happen. It was a small thing but seemed huge at the time. On reflection most of life is made up of small things and if we do not exercise faith in each of them and draw every event into a faith walk with God, huge sections of life and time will be lived in our own strength and by our own wisdom. We would then live just like the world instead of being the supernatural people we are in God.

We discovered that to have faith is simply to obey what God says. The act of obedience reveals what the Bible calls faith. To use another word, it is simply trusting God; trusting what He says. As we continued to obey we found that our ability to trust God grew. We discovered that faith is not learned in one lesson and unfortunately, lessons learned can soon be forgotten. We developed a determined attitude to just trust and obey when God spoke, either through His word or as whispered guidance in our spirits. Through these simple steps a lifestyle of faith was established.

CHAPTER 11

WILL ANYONE SEND US?

We prayed and examined the information we received from the Bible and Medical Missionary Fellowship (BMMF) and decided to fill in the long forms and apply. (Today the mission is called Interserve.) There were so many questions such as "Have you had consumption?" "How many miles can you walk?" The application forms belonged to another era! We wrote our testimonies telling why we wished to be missionaries. After these papers had been considered we were called for interviews with various people and committees. One refined godly lady took me aside and in hushed shocked tones said, "My dear, you don't mean to say you have been in the world!?" She was so unaccustomed to interviewing someone from a non-Christian home.

The next formality was a medical examination. I passed; I had always had good health. But it was a different story for Alan and our application came to a halt. He could not say that any of the treatments he had received in many hospital visits had brought any permanent healing. He still had continuous heavy bleeding and could lose more than a pint of blood at a time. During this period of our application, Alan became so anemic, that on one occasion he had four pints of blood by transfusion. His pallor and lack of any physical strength, told its own story. The slightest exertion was almost too much for him. Emergency visits to the hospital became too common.

As you can imagine, the Doctor's report sent back to the missionary society was not very favorable. Kindly, they suggested that Alan seek further medical advice. Again he was admitted to the hospital for more investigations and minor operations. But nothing seemed to help; in fact his condition was deteriorating. Again we were wondering why the Lord didn't heal. Was the Lord saying we should not go? We did all we could to fulfill the requirements of BMMF but Alan's health problems continued to stand in the way of our acceptance. The final letter from BMMF recognized the genuineness of our call to foreign missions, but suggested that we work on the home end of the mission, echoing the words of the medical advice, "So that you can stay near to medical help." We had arrived at yet another impasse. Would any mission society ever send us? We needed a healing miracle and that was not happening, though we prayed and believed as best as we could.

In the summer of 1962, we went for a week's holiday. Rachel was two years old and already a very strong-willed character. She didn't enjoy playing on the stony beach or paddling in the cold sea. She felt cooped up in the small house and frustrated in the car. At the end of the lane was a field of cows which fortunately entranced her. So day after day we walked to the gate and stood while Rachel said, "Moo" and then I said, "Yes dear, moo!" We were all bored with holiday activities; the uppermost thought in our minds was how to get to India.

Alan had been having a spasmodic correspondence with Bill Thompson of Gospel Literature Service Press in Bombay. Over the months it had become clear that we should be planning to join them in the early part of the following year, 1963. We had hoped that we would able to go under the auspices of BMMF. We struggled with the thought that no missionary society would ever send us, but the more we prayed the clearer it seemed the Lord was saying, "Go anyway".

One evening Alan went for a walk along the moonlit beach. He had many big questions in his mind. "Lord if You are calling me to go, why don't You heal me? It's so simple for You to heal me." That evening the Lord had called Alan to the beach for a very special purpose. The Lord had questions for Alan that scoured the depths of his heart. That night he was forced again to face the basic issue of his lack of trust, as the Lord painfully went over the same ground he had dealt with a year before, during his hospital stay. The Lord said, "Alan, if Kodak was to send you to India would you go?"

"Lord, of course, they are a reputable company. They have been in business a long time and would care for me in every way."

"But Alan, I've been in business longer than Kodak. If the missionary society was to send you, would you go?"

"Yes Lord, I know they would provide for us."

"But can't you trust Me?"

Alan spent a long time in prayer on the beach. When he came back, his mind was made up. Yes, he would trust the Lord. We would go. With the decision made, we hoped and wondered if the Lord would heal Alan before we went. We waited expectantly everyday hoping for an improvement. After a few weeks of frequent bleeding, it became obvious that the Lord was not going to heal just then.

It seemed right to ask the missionary society once more if they would send us as we were. Kindly, they reconsidered our application and Alan was seen by an eminent specialist. His report came back, "It would be an unjustifiable risk to proceed with his application for missionary service overseas." Very sympathetically, they wrote to us assuming all thought of foreign service would now be far from us and suggested again, that we help the mission at the home end. When the letter came it was no surprise. The Lord had already prepared us for the decision and we knew that we would go as the Lord opened the way.

Calmly, we considered our position. Our circle of Christian friends was very small. We lived in a small community, went to the local Baptist church who had one missionary overseas with the Baptist Missionary Society. Her name was rarely mentioned from year to year. We knew nobody who had any fervent missionary vision and no one with money who could send us and very few people who would continue to remember us in prayer. Our prayer was, "Lord if You are sending us now, provide for us now."

CHAPTER 12

SETTING THE COURSE

During the next two months the Lord clarified many issues in our minds. When eventually it became clear that the Lord was leading us to go to India in February the following year, we were already half-way through November. Even so the decision was easily made. We had peace; the Lord had chosen the date. We would sail to Bombay, India in just four months' time, in February 1963 to work with the Gospel Literature Service Press in Bombay. We knew the days would come when our call would be challenged, so we were asking God for tangible proof that He was with us every step of the way. We did not wish to send ourselves by using our own limited finances so we asked the Lord for supernatural provision. We prayed and expected financial gifts. Already our families viewed our actions as very unwise, especially as I was pregnant with our third child, who would now be born in India! Rachel was two years old.

Drawing upon the lessons learned from many great Christian biographies, it was plain to us that we should ask no one for anything, but wait for the Lord to provide. In this manner, we knew the Lord could directly control our timing. We lived as those getting ready to sail, although we had no tangible evidence that this would be so. We covenanted with the Lord to book our passage immediately when we received a gift for that purpose, however small.

As we prepared to go, we counted every day wondering when the Lord would step in and say, "Now is the time, book your passage!" On November 26th, Alan went to visit a business colleague, Jim, whom he had recently led to Christ. Jim knew our burning ambition to go to India and in the course of the evening said he was gathering money together to send us! Alan came home with the news and we prayed,

"Lord, this is not money in the hand, but is it the signal to go to the shipping agent and at least make enquiries?" We decided that it was.

The next day Alan visited the local travel agent. The assistant was quite nonplussed by his request. Not many people wanted a boat sailing to India in February. After all her enquiries she could only offer us a sailing in March. We knew that wasn't the right time, the Lord had said "Go in February." We left the problem with the agent who would make further enquiries.

We were confident the Lord had given us the signal to move ahead. The time had come for resolute decisions. Alan gave his resignation to Kodak; his colleagues were shocked at his decision. A few days later the telephone rang in Alan's office. On the line was the personal secretary to the Chairman of the Board of Directors. "The Chairman would like to meet you for lunch. Will you please be at the Kingsway office on Wednesday at 12.30 p.m.?"

Alan put the telephone down and repeated the message to himself. He could hardly believe it. "Lunch with the Chairman" he whispered. Wednesday came; he found himself half running up Kingsway to get to the office on time. The train had been delayed. It was already 12.30 p.m. He was late. As he entered the office, the Chairman was making for the door pulling on his overcoat. Obviously he did not intend to wait for his late guest. Brushing aside Alan's lame apologies, he introduced Kodak's legal adviser who was also to join them for lunch.

As the meal proceeded the two men questioned Alan closely on his reason for resigning. They talked to him in a kindly concerned way, as a father would reason with an irresponsible son. They were obviously intrigued that one of their senior men, who had such good prospects, should recklessly throw it all away to become a missionary with no apparent means of financial support.

They listened intently as Alan told them the story of his conversion and how he knew God was calling him to go to India. They realized he could not be dissuaded, so counseled him to make proper provision for his family and to look for some security. They assumed Alan was passing through a phase and would eventually see reason and return to a normal life.

The Chairman said he would cable Bombay and arrange for reliable employment for Alan. This he did. (As soon as we arrived in Bombay, Alan was called for an interview.) Besides this, the Kodak Manager in Bombay was told, "Keep an eye upon them" should they find themselves in trouble.

Alan glanced at his watch and was surprised to see that it was three o'clock. These busy Kodak executives had lost count of time as they were confronted with a living faith. Rising from the table the Chairman said rather wistfully, "Look at our lives, they don't really account for much. There are at least a dozen men waiting to step into my shoes. Perhaps you are doing the right thing after all."

We were learning that being a missionary is primarily being the kind of person who witnesses to Jesus Christ in any situation and at every opportunity; crossing the sea wasn't going to make us into missionaries. The nearer we got to sailing the more clearly we saw that witnessing in our present life was our missionary training. Alan had long ago got over his shyness of speaking of Christ and now in an unabashed manner, with his loud clear voice, he would speak to anybody anywhere.

When Rachel was born my life became demanding; no longer did I have time for visiting friends or arranging coffee mornings for preaching the gospel. The daily visit to the shops at the bottom of our hill became my evangelistic opportunity. I laugh now as I remember that as I pushed the pram down the hill, I would sing "Guide me Oh! Thou great Jehovah," expecting the Lord to send across my path those to whom I could speak of Christ. It made going to buy a loaf of bread quite exciting; each day I wondered what the Lord would do!

Another group of evangelistic opportunities were the tradesmen who called at the door. One day the window cleaner, a genial man, came whistling round to the back door. As I filled his bucket with water, the Lord said to me, "You can speak to this man." "But how Lord? What to say? He is only talking about the weather." The window cleaner went off to do his job and I hurried away upstairs to have this out with the Lord. I took my Bible asking Him to show me what to say and how to begin. I was on my knees by my bed when I heard the window cleaner's ladder bang against the bedroom window. Hurriedly I jumped up and went to the next room till I was driven from there again by the thump of the ladder. I cried to God to show me how to begin the conversation with this man. Opening the Bible my eyes fell upon, "Open your mouth and I will fill it." I could have laughed, but really I felt more like crying. For some reason, and I don't know why, that day I hadn't the courage to begin a spiritual conversation from nothing. Feeling hounded, I went downstairs clutching my Bible.

Soon his task was completed. When he came to collect his money I was kneeling on the kitchen floor. I went prayerfully to the door wondering how to detain him long enough to speak to him. All I had to guide me, was what seemed to be a very unhelpful scripture. Handing him his money, I deliberately opened my mouth and expected God to fill it just as He had said He would! After the first few sentences I found myself with great ease telling this elderly man how Jesus could be his Savior. He listened intently and said, "No one has ever told me these things before." After he left, I praised God, "Lord You spoke to him, You opened his heart to hear, make me more obedient to Your voice." Sadly, two weeks later I read in the obituary column of the local paper that my window cleaner had suddenly died. I wished I could say that I knew he received the Lord, but the timing was sobering. How I thanked God that I had been obedient.

A few days later on December 3rd, I went to speak to the Women's meeting in the Baptist Chapel in the nearby village of Chipperfield. The congregation was a faithful group of ladies who met weekly for a short message followed by tea and biscuits. As I prayed about my message only one thing burned in me. I told them my testimony; how I had been converted and that I was going to India in February as a missionary. I stated it as a fact, though we were still waiting for the money to make the booking for the February sailing.

As I spoke, heads nodded with approval and the precious faces responded sympathetically. It was a rare thing to hear of people going oversees as missionaries and it was even more poignant as I was obviously pregnant, that evoked many questions. Afterwards I sat with the secretary to drink a cup of tea and eat a Marie biscuit when a beaming old lady, huddled up in her winter coat came to talk to me. She introduced herself, "I'm Mrs. Smith", and then she pressed five shillings into my hand. "My dear, I have had the privilege of being the first person to send a missionary before and I want to do it again. Please accept this small gift to send you to India." It was as if I had received the widow's mite; Mrs. Smith was living on a government pension and I knew that left her with no spare money.

An unspeakable joy and thankfulness flooded my heart. On the homeward journey the car seemed to fly up and down the hills. I couldn't get into the house quickly enough to show Alan the precious five shillings. Though it was a very small gift, it was the key to unlock all that we would require. We prayed and rejoiced, "Lord You are real, You have heard our prayers. You are the instigator of all we are doing. It is Your voice that we have heard and obeyed. Oh Lord we love You!"

That evening we were like small children; this gift of money in our hands was the sign we had waited for. We were so excited. Just the day before we had received notice that berths were available on a ship sailing in February. The five shillings was the seal, we now knew this was our ship. As soon as possible Alan confirmed the bookings.

CHAPTER 13

MORE TRIALS AND MORE FAITH

A few days later we came down to earth with a bump. A bill for sixty pounds arrived for the deposit on our passage. We looked at the bill and wondered, were we to pay it ourselves? Then the Lord said, "You are not to use any of your own money but watch and see what I will do." The Lord must have overheard our thinking. We needed to be one hundred percent certain that we were not sending ourselves. The way ahead would have many difficulties. Alan was still bleeding profusely and frequently needed help. If we were putting ourselves into the way of trouble, we had to know that it was all part of God's perfect will.

Usually we tried to pay all our bills within ten days of receipt, so we applied the same rule to this bill. We fixed a date ten days hence and expected that by some means God would provide the sixty pounds by that Friday. For the first few days nothing happened. How we prayed! The following Tuesday the Lord said He would send money that day. We believed and waited expectantly. Alan left for work as usual. The postman walked straight past the house with the first mail delivery, a few hours later I was again at the window hoping to see him bring the second delivery. Soon it was obvious that there was nothing for us. I banished my disappointment by assuring myself that the Lord wasn't dependent upon the postal service. I began to dream up other ways in which I thought He could provide for us that day. When Alan arrived home I was waiting for him feeling quite sure that he would have been given a gift at work, but no, he had nothing. As we ate our evening meal we encouraged each other to continue to believe that the Lord had said we would have a gift that day.

We had been greatly influenced by the lives of people like George Müller of Bristol and in a like manner we were not making our needs known, asking for money or even giving hints or suggestions to anyone. This was a spiritual exercise between us and God. We viewed it as an experiment; was that God speaking to us or just our own imagination? Was God really saying He would send us money today? We never heard an audible voice, the Holy Spirit had spoken in our spirits, though never more than an impression, or was it imagination? The inward voice persisted even when all outward evidence seemed contrary. Because what we heard could be denied, it was easy to question, examine and doubt, but that day we chose to believe. The Lord was teaching us the ways of faith.

Alan left that evening to attend the weekly prayer meeting at the church. In our natural thinking this seemed to be the last remaining opportunity of the day for us to receive a gift. But we were limiting the Lord! My ears were hyper sensitive to any click of the letter box so I was immediately on my feet as I heard a letter plop to the floor. I picked up the envelope and ripped it open, inside were two pounds and a hand written note with Philippians 4:19. "My God shall supply all your need according to His riches in glory by Christ Jesus." The donor left quickly on a motor bike and although I tried to work out who it could be, we never knew. All I could do was praise the Lord, we had heard His voice and He had heard our prayers.

Having received no gift from anyone at the prayer meeting, Alan hurried home puzzled, but still believing. As he walked up the hill he thought to himself, *"I was so sure the Lord was going to give us a gift today that I could have stood in the doorway with my hand out!"* I could hardly wait for him to get in the house. Excitedly I greeted him with the envelope; the tangible evidence of our faith. How we praised the Lord. It was such a small thing but at the same time, such a big thing. Great faith, like a journey is accomplished one step at a time. Every victory where God's voice is believed against doubts, delays and impossibilities builds faith in our hearts. I like to think of it as building a wall; each possession of faith is like a brick, and great faith like a wall, takes many bricks!

Though very thankful for the two pounds, we still needed fifty-eight pounds and the deadline was Friday. This first test was so crucial; we had to know that God was sending us. We prayed and continued to wait for Him, telling no one of our need. In the natural there was no reason why anyone would ever give us money as we must have appeared to most people, to be very comfortably placed. Yet small sums of money were given, each one a surprise and most came in the last few days just before our deadline and each gift was a huge encouragement. God was hearing our prayers. When Friday came we had received sixty-three pounds, mainly from people unknown to us. The final gift that took us over the sixty pound target came just one hour before our 5:00 p.m. deadline! Yes God is never early, but He is never late! How we praised Him. We were going to India in the will of the Lord and He was taking responsibility for us and in His own miraculous manner, He would supply all our needs.

With carefully prepared lists we took stock of what we actually needed to get us to India. I sat on the floor with sheets of paper scattered about me, while Alan totaled up what appeared to us a huge sum of money. We were very despondent as we realized we would need at least £500. It seemed an impossible amount. We had no joy that afternoon as we faced the stark reality of our situation. But we couldn't turn back. God had led us this far and with our little faith we believed He would see us through. He comforted us from His word with promises of provision, and said, "Behold I come suddenly; and those who believe will not be put to shame!" Telling the story some time later in a prayer letter from India, after many miracles of provision, I said, "We had no idea how the Lord would provide and it was a great thrill for us to see Him work it all out with such precision to the very last pound." We even began to enjoy our impossible situation! It wasn't of our own making; the Lord had led us this way and it was becoming very exciting. At times we were so detached from our circumstances that we had not a care in the world. We would look at ourselves with amazement.

Our plans to go to India meant we had to evaluate everything we owned. Did we keep it, sell it or give it away? Most surplus items were given away, but then the big question filled our thinking for days and days. What should we do with our home? The wisest option seemed to be— sell the house, we did not want the burden of owning a property and having to find the money for the mortgage each quarter. As we made enquiries we had a definite check in our spirits; the Lord showed us that He had plans for our home. It unfolded that the Lord wanted us to keep the house and to make it available to missionary families on home leave. We learned how difficult it was for those with large families to find the right accommodation. Located conveniently for travel into London or anywhere else in the nation and with four large bedrooms, our home, The Elms, was perfect for the purpose.

Once we came into agreement with the Lord's plan we were presented with a new set of challenges, all requiring new levels of faith. We had not lived in The Elms for very long and the rooms were not fully furnished so as to be adequate for a large family. The few gifts that came were now needed to buy furniture and other essentials for missionary families that we presumed would come to stay. Would these same families be able to cover the mortgage payments? We never knew. Our faith was being stretched beyond anything we envisaged when all this began.

I imagined the rooms filled with children, so I busied myself gathering bed linens, blankets and as well as extra beds, baby cots and every conceivable thing, from extra knives and forks, to table cloths. As we informed missionary societies about the availability of our home they were enthusiastic telling us that there was a very real need. This undertaking became a huge faith project in itself and as we drew near to our sailing date the burden was overwhelming.

So much work went into preparing the home that it was very disappointing when despite our making it available to various missions we had no confirmed tenants. The New Year came and we thought surely there would be a family ready to move in as soon as when we left. The specter of our home standing empty and the property deteriorating with no income for the mortgage taunted us. We were still asking the Lord for the final payment for our sailing and now this. On every front our faith was being tried. *"Are we crazy? Is this really what the Lord wants?"* My father came to help us with some practical things and he did not hide his disapproval of all we were doing. He did think we were crazy and reminded us that soon we would have a new baby.

CHAPTER 14

SAILING DAY

It was only eight short weeks from our sailing date, so taking our formidable list we began to buy the things we required for ourselves, as well as items for the home. Soon the few gifts we had received during Christmas were spent and we had nothing left to save for our passage. It seemed that the Lord had forgotten about us. Each day we looked for the mail waiting for miracles but nothing happened. Fortunately the shipping line had not sent the bill for the balance of the money we owed as they had not been able to confirm me as a passenger. I would be twenty-seven weeks pregnant by the time I joined the ship and regulations required that the ship's surgeon make the decision about my travel. We continued spending any gifts we received assuming that when the fare was required, the money would come.

The local newspaper interviewed us and printed our story just as we told them. As we read it through we thought, *"Lord we are utterly cast upon You, You can't fail us now. Alan has no job and so far we have no confirmed sailing date or the money for the passage."* Our situation seemed so unreal. We were not going to churches telling our story or preaching; we were unknown except to our immediate circle. Looking at our situation from a natural point of view, it was quite unreasonable for us to expect to receive money in answer to prayer. No one would ever think we needed it, but we had grown in faith; we knew it was impossible for God to fail. There were times when a sneaking fear would grip our hearts, but deep down the revelation of God's faithfulness was rock solid; we knew that what God had said He would do.

After a week of no gifts and huge impossibilities, suddenly things changed with no explicable reason. Money started coming, first twenty pounds, then twenty-five, then thirty. We were rejoicing, but still my travel was not finalized and we had the remainder of the fare to pay. Our heavy luggage had already been shipped to the dock in Liverpool; our goods had gone before us.

It was just two weeks before sailing day. At the kitchen table that memorable Saturday morning a miracle happened. Two letters arrived, we quickly open the first one from the shipping line; yes they approved of my sailing, but with the good news also came the bill of almost £200.00; money we did not have. The second letter was from India. Tearing it open, Alan drew out a letter and inside was a folded check for £200! An English lady, unknown to us and living at that time in India, had heard of our imminent travel and wanted to assist us on our journey. What rejoicing there was in the kitchen that morning. Only the Lord could have so arranged for the bill and the check to arrive together. Our God is a God of miracles and He is always faithful to His Word.

Despite the overwhelming evidence of God's hand upon our lives, our days were clouded by Alan's continual bleeding. He was very weak. He looked an ashen color as he stood to speak at our farewell meeting in the church. At one time I thought the Lord spoke to me from the story of the ten lepers, "As they went, they were healed." I wanted to believe; perhaps I just hoped that it would be so for Alan. He had no reason to think that medical science could help him. His condition had only deteriorated, despite many doctors' treatments. Alan was firmly trusting God to heal, but that healing did not come for many years. The Lord allowed that weakening condition to teach us many things.

There were times when his bleeding was so profuse that I could not stop it. I thought his life would just slip away. Our last night in England was one of those occasions. The final things were packed; the suitcases were in the hall waiting for the morning. Precious Rachel was asleep upstairs in her own bed for the last time and we sat for a moment reflecting on the path we were taking. Suddenly, I was jolted back to present reality— the little new life within me made his presence felt. Then, Alan started to bleed. It was gushing! Despite my well-practiced ability at packing his nose, the bleeding would not stop. Tipping out the second large basin full of Alan's lifeblood it seemed the enemy was mocking us. In a last ditch ferocious attack, he threw everything he could at us. I felt helpless;

whatever I did Alan continued bleeding and he would not hear of going to the hospital, we had walked this way dozens of times before. I was in agony watching him as he was near to fainting with the loss of blood. Praying and rebuking the enemy, I told the Lord, "I'm determined, I will not give in". Biting back my tears I said, "Lord even if I have to go to India as a widow, I go. You called me, I will follow You."

The following day, Alan could barely carry a suitcase as we boarded the train to Liverpool. Our dear friends from the Bible and Medical Missionary Fellowship, who had seen us this far, were at the station in London to see us off and I knew we were in their prayers.

That day as we walked out of The Elms to go to India, there were no definite plans for the future of the house. It became the biggest burden of all. I hardly dared to think what my father would say. We had deliberately shut the front door and left it to God as we walked away, taking agonizing steps of faith. We encouraged ourselves, surely it was the Lord who had led us to prepare the home for missionary families, but my family didn't understand and were very distressed.

A good friend had instructions to sell the property if we ran out of money, but in the mean time we would wait. How hard it was to wait. About this time I wrote to my sister, "We do not understand and I know it looks so irresponsible, but God is in control. He will not mock us for doing what we believe to be His will." Assuring her I said, "You will never know that God is the God of the impossible, until you find yourself in an impossible situation."

The ship steamed out from Liverpool dock on a bitterly cold February day in 1963; the nation was blanketed in deep snow. Clutching my coat about me and shielding Rachel from the biting wind, we waved goodbye to my sister, standing alone on the quay side. We were on our way to India. Our berths had been reserved and paid for by the King of Kings. We were His ambassadors.

Eileen at five years old.

Eileen when a student nurse.

Alan a new recruit in the
Royal Air Force, 18 years old.

Eileen at age 15.

CHRISTIANS FOR ONLY FOUR YEARS

Langley Family Now Take Up Missionary Work

FIVE years ago Mr. Alan Vincent and his wife Eileen had never been to church. Their only Bible was gathering dust in the attic. But in a fortnight's time they leave their home in Langley-hill, Kings Langley, and sail to India, where Mr. Vincent will voluntarily devote his specialist knowledge to the extension of a Christian printing press in Bombay and where his wife will take up mission work.

A section of the article that appeared in the Kings Langley Times, Feb 1963.

Alan and Eileen in Calcutta at Carey Baptist Church.

Bill and Dorothy Thompson, who
opened their home to us in Bombay.

At the Thompson's house learning how to buy vegetables with
Daya the servant 1963.

Satnam Palace, Bombay. Our first home in Bombay.

The family in Bombay October 1963.

The Byculla Market, Bombay.

Bombay Baptist Church where the
Holy Spirit fell in 1965.

The Rev. David McKee used of God to
bring revival in Bombay.

Biswanath and Vijaya Chowdhuri outside the
Discipleship Center they founded in Dhaka, Bangladesh.

Alan teaching in Nepal.

Bombay during the Ganpati festival.

John Babu with Alan in the early days
of establishing Sion Fellowship.

John Babu and his Family in 1978.

Preaching in the villages of Andhra Pradesh.

The Triumph Herald, the Miracle Car.

Rachel standing under the main entrance of
Hebron School 1000 miles from Bombay.

Rachel and Duncan ready for Hebron School.

The beginning of the church in Chuim 1970.

Catholic festival in Chuim outside our home.

Eileen counseling a young lady in Nepal.

Alan healed from years of debilitating bleeding.

The family before leaving India 1974.

CHAPTER 15

LIVING IN A PALACE

Bill Thompson met us at the ship as we docked in Bombay. He impressed us with his genial and efficient manner. He wasted no time and as landing formalities were being completed, he was outlining the needs of Gospel Literature Service to Alan and analyzing his ability to help.

We must have looked a very disappointing couple, Alan was thin and drawn. He had continued to bleed profusely during our voyage and both he and Rachel had suffered severely with sea sickness. Bill listened carefully as we unfolded yet another drama in our lives.

When the ship had left Aden, a port city in Yemen, the enemy turned his attack upon me. I went into premature labor. It seemed the baby was going to be born before we arrived in Bombay! The ship's surgeon did all he could to reassure us, saying that at twenty-eight weeks pregnant, the baby was strong and viable. He even constructed a make-shift oxygen tent out of plastic sheeting and a drawer and was ready for a premature birth. The baby was coming.

When I became pregnant, the Lord told me I was carrying a boy. I had cried out to the Lord, "Oh God, give me a revivalist!" So we named the expected child Duncan, after the revivalist Duncan Campbell. That night lying on the bunk in the ship's hospital, I turned my face to the wall. I was in torment. There are promises on this child's life. He must live. How could this be? Ringing in my ears were the words spoken as I left England, "You fool, you lost your first boy and you will lose this one too." Talking to the Lord in my anguish, I said, "If that is the truth and I lose this boy, I will still obey You. I will go to India, nothing will stop me." I prayed, "The Lord gives and the Lord takes away, blessed be the Name of the Lord!"

Two seasoned missionaries on board joined Alan praying continuously that my labor would stop. The next port of call was Karachi, Pakistan where the ship's doctor wanted to admit me into the city hospital. I only managed to avoid that fate by the Lord's intervention in answer to prayer. The contractions began to subside and the doctor said as long as I was lying down and resting Duncan was safe. I can't imagine what Bill thought as he listened to this catalogue of events.

Despite our weak state and exhausted appearance we were so thankful to be in Bombay at last. Four years had passed since the Lord had first said, "Go to India," but it was less than ten weeks since we had received the first gift to send us. "Lo, I come suddenly," is a very apt word for guidance.

We lived with the Thompson family for three months, while we waited for the baby to be born. It was a privilege to be with them; they taught us the first steps of how to live in India. The first few days in their rambling flat were spent lying on the hard bed listening to all the noises flooding through the open windows. Crows fought and squawked at each other almost drowning out the voices of all kinds of vendors, each with his own special call. Then there was a strange plunking noise that I thought was some kind of musical instrument, only to find that it was a contraption for teasing out hardened cotton mattresses! There was never a moment of quiet; all the windows were permanently open to catch whatever little breeze found its way through the closely packed buildings.

Dorothy Thompson was an amazing mother of five children and mother to all who were in need. One morning a young woman visited. She had just come from the local public hospital where she had given birth to a tiny baby girl that weighed less than two pounds. There were no facilities to care for premature babies, so the little one had been left on a side shelf to die. Dorothy was comforting and loving the young mother, but my mind went into a whirl. *"Lord does life have so little value?"* I wondered what kind of society I had come to. My baby would soon be born, what was I to expect?

Both Alan and I found our first months difficult with the heat, strange food, adjusting to a totally different culture, not having a home of our own and most of all seeing Rachel very distressed by all the changes. I regained strength and was able to lead a more normal life. The weeks passed quickly and right on time Duncan entered into this life, a healthy full term boy. How we all praised God. His precious life had been spared. Now all he had to contend with was Bombay in the hot season and colic!

Duncan's arrival signaled the time for us to spread our wings and leave the loving care of Dorothy and Bill. Not only had they shared their flat with us for three months, but they had shared their meager water supply. Each dribble from the tap was precious. During our stay we had learned valuable lessons to help us in the next phase of Bombay life; now we would be facing many challenges including our own very acute water shortages.

Alan had been continually bleeding for the three months we had been in India. The merciless heat during the hot season added to the burden of his weakness. Alan, with an indomitable spirit and an oversized sense of responsibility, would not give in, stay home, take the morning off, or any such thing; even if in his sleep he had soaked his pillow with blood and felt ill. Obviously this was a cause of huge concern to Bill Thompson, so he introduced Alan to a Christian doctor, who was the supervisor for a large public hospital. In the course of conversation she said she needed a good tenant for her new flat. This was a major answer to prayer. The Lord knew our need, so now that we were ready to move, the place was provided. Again we were reminded of the words of Mr. Elliott, our first mentor, who used to say in his strong Midlands accent, "Know this lad, God is never early but He is never late!"

I wondered where we were being taken to when Bill turned off a noisy main road down an alley way. All about us were tall tenement buildings five or six floors high. They looked as if they had never seen paint and were in desperate need of a wash! Following Bill, we stepped over water pipes where rats scurried. Hungry cats turned a blind eye; they were waiting for tasty scraps to plop down from the upper windows. Disregarding the stares we were receiving from every opening, we went into a new building called, Satnam Palace. It appeared to have nudged its way into the 'higgledy-piggledy' maze of buildings. We looked at the tiny elevator; it was not working so we took to the stairs. The 'Palace' was not so palatial and didn't deserve such a name. We stepped over trash and squashed food as we made our way up the dirty steps!

Before leaving England I had prayed for a small house and garden so that the children would have somewhere to play. Now I realized such was impossible. We had come to view a flat on the fifth floor, with just five hundred square feet. Later we learnt how fortunate we were to have such accommodation in a city where so little was available.

Standing for a moment in the empty three roomed flat with its stone floors and whitewashed walls, we looked around taking it all in. Bill flung open the windows and to our surprise we saw directly into our neighbors' bedrooms, kitchens, and living rooms. Wherever we looked out, we were looking in on someone else's life and obviously the converse was true. Open windows were essential to catch the welcome breath of wind, as in most homes there was no air conditioning. Every activity in our small rooms was under scrutiny by curious eyes. Laughing we said, "We could lean over from our balcony to the next building and fasten our neighbor's shirt buttons!" Looking at each other we said to Bill, "Yes, this is wonderful, this will do for us," so ended the wearisome search for somewhere to live. Mission life for us, was not in a grass hut, but in a tenement building in a city that never slept. It was almost impossible to rent anywhere without paying huge bribes. *Pugery,* as it was called, controlled all deals and without paying up, little happened. Bill negotiated the flat for us and both he and the Christian owner would have nothing to do with bribes, this added to our confidence, it was an answer to our prayers.

Duncan was nine days old when we moved our few trunks into Satnam Palace and started to set up home. We were happy as familiar objects were placed about the room, each awakening nostalgic memories of another life. Squeals of delight came from Rachel rummaging in the packing cases, as she rediscovered her toys. Now this was home, but we could hardly imagine what the future would hold.

The Englishman's home is his castle, but not so in India where our flat seemed to be the latest tourist attraction! We were a huge source of interest to our neighbors who besides watching everything we did through our windows, would want to come into our little haven to examine everything and I mean everything! They would look at the furniture and how we organized the kitchen; our fair children were of greatest interest and a delight to all, but Rachel did not appreciate having her face pinched by every admiring person.

We lived in the constant hubbub of raised voices and the incessant blaring of radios blasting us with the latest Indian pop song. Then there was always the thundering traffic, to which our ears slowly became dulled. Clouds of sickly, smelling incense frequently wafted up from the flats below as the Hindus worshipped their gods or tried to ward off evil spirits. The majority of the occupants seemed to have a western outlook, so initially this kind of worship seemed incongruous to us. As we became more familiar with our environment, to our surprise, we discovered that even highly educated people would bow to an idol.

A shout came from the kitchen, "Run! Shut the windows!" The torrential rain was pouring in over my bed. The monsoon had arrived. There was nothing genteel about this rain, no gentle showers, the clouds opened up and dropped a deluge upon us as if buckets were being emptied overhead! Since we lived on the top floor and the room was very small and the windows were never closed, it only took a few moments for our beds to be drenched.

Quickly I learned what to do in a monsoon. Its effects were far ranging; baby Duncan broke out in prickly heat, an irritating rash I had never seen before. The poor child was very distressed as it covered his whole body and then erupted into boils. I was amazed that the clothes hanging in the cupboard grew mildew, and if a pair of shoes were untouched for a time they would be green and fuzzy. When the sun broke through, the wet streets would steam. In the humidity so much sweat just ran from our bodies so that at times I thought something was walking up my legs, but it was only sweat running down. As the rain fell in sheets, the sweeper people who made a living by doing the most menial of jobs and considered the lowest in the Hindu caste system retreated to living in doorways. The *wallas* who sold and repaired sunglasses changed their occupation to the repair of umbrellas.

My visit to the doctor on a very rainy day turned out to be a lesson in flood management. It had rained for hours. Bombay is built upon islands and the city's drains run out into the sea. That afternoon was high tide and the pressure it created shut off all drainage from the flooding streets. The torrential rain had nowhere to go. When I came out of the doctor's office there were no streets to be seen. I began to wade through the flood that came up to my knees, following the crowd to higher ground. All the time I was hoping I would not be swept away in one of the open drains!

Satnam Palace was a place full of interest. It was always noisy with an assortment of wonderful smells of cooking, but in the monsoon, the predominant smell was rotting garbage! As the building was owned by Muslims it attracted a large number of Muslim tenants. Our neighbor decided to take another younger wife and there was a huge celebration to which we were invited. We didn't know what the etiquette was for such an event. On the occasion of Ramadan, blaring loudspeakers and decorations festooned the roof for the festivities. Rachel came running into the flat shouting, "Mummy, Mummy there is blood on the stars, they are killing a goat!"

Down below the building lived a family of sweepers, rolling out their bedding on the concrete at night and cooking meals on a paraffin burner by day. One day the mother came to my door and presented me with her baby, its toe had been bitten off by a rat in the night! On another occasion, when the whole family was badly infected with scabies, she came for help and I walked with them to the public hospital, about a mile away, to get treatment. The doctor was only too happy to give me the task of their daily treatment, so my kitchen became a clinic.

Opportunities to share about Jesus presented themselves continually. One day, two Kashmiri Muslims came to the flat selling carved wood. We bought a few things and shared the gospel, but in a short while the young boy returned alone asking that we would tell him more of Jesus. It was wonderful to lead him to salvation. Our tiny flat was an outpost of Heaven from where we were continually reaching out to the lost. When the place was crammed with students asking questions and listening to testimonies, the neighbors would look in and wonder what we were doing. There were plenty of opportunities to tell them. Even the joy on our faces prompted enquiries, "Why are you so happy?" Then, how easy it was to talk about Jesus. Satnam Palace became a wonderful home and a place where we were baptized into ordinary Indian life.

CHAPTER 16

BOMBAY UP CLOSE AND PERSONAL

Strolling in the afternoons to do the shopping, I was amazed at the teeming crowds; there were people everywhere. It seemed as if each day was the last minute Christmas rush, except the people were not shoving and pushing in a hurry, these were ambling along, sitting or even sleeping. There were mangy dogs, skinny cats, children in all stages of undress and stark naked toddlers, except for a black thread tied round their tummies to ward off the evil eye. In every conceivable nook and cranny, there was a family living, eating and sleeping.

The first impressions of Bombay are deeply embedded in our memories. The city was vibrant; a bustling place full of noise, smells, people, animals and holes in the road! Cars were driven with one hand on the horn, squeals from brakes indicated that someone had had to yield in the battle of the road. Mixed up in the traffic chaos were bullock carts traveling at two miles per hour. Sacred cows wandered at a regal pace. Others sat and chewed the cud wherever the fancy took them and were quite oblivious to vehicles inching past as if they were negotiating an extra traffic island. Cows sent out to scavenge wandered about in small herds. They rummaged in the rubbish tips for tasty scraps and contentedly munched up plastic bags and newspapers. Commuters made room for them as they sheltered from the rain and heat at the bus stands.

Pedestrians, whom I am sure had suicidal tendencies, darted between honking trucks. The hundreds of taxis and double decked buses were driven as if no one else was on the road. Interlacing their way sedately through this battlefield, were the most dilapidated old horse drawn carriages, which looked as if they had just come straight from the Victoria and Albert Museum in London. The atmosphere was laden with suffocating petrol fumes, the stench of drains and the farmyard smell of fresh animal manure to the sublime heavy perfumes of exotic flower laden trees.

One hot afternoon I wandered with the lethargic crowd to the large road junction at the corner where we lived. I usually bought eggs from a man who squatted there on the steps of a cheap eating house with the basket between his knees. Among the vehicles jostling for position at the traffic lights, were three men with a handcart piled high with potatoes for the market. They only had a short distance to go, but it was up a steep incline over the railway bridge. The lights changed to green. The men tried to get their burden rolling. The leader, with a holster round his shoulders, strained as he pulled with all his might, yelling at the other men to push. The cart unwillingly moved. The muscles stood out in sharp relief on the men's skinny bodies. Their naked backs looked oiled as the sweat poured from them, soaking their thin loin cloths. There was no actual whip to drive these men like beasts of burden, they were driven by their desperate need to provide for their families the basics of life. One of the small wheels of the hand cart stuck in a pot hole, the load lurched, the men struggled with every ounce of their energy, but the cart would not move. The lights changed and with a roar the traffic rushed upon them; the policeman on duty yelled, cursing and swearing. Their faces were weary with exhaustion as they heaved their load out of the way. Inside I was crying for them. I wanted to help push, I could not bear to see God's precious creation brought lower than the animals. The three men collapsed on the curb with their heads in their hands. Bullocks trotted by unperturbed dragging their loads.

Crossing the road with the baby's stroller was no simple matter. Besides the traffic, there were always pot holes that during the flooded conditions of the monsoon added to the adventure. Before stepping off the footpath, I would gingerly prod the swirling water in the gutter with my umbrella to make sure I wasn't walking into an open drain. This was no idle fear, for at one time as Alan ran for a bus, he saw a man in the flooded street step into an open manhole right up to his thigh.

Besides the unintentional holes there were numerous excavations by various municipal departments. Some appeared to have been forgotten, while others were a seething mass of people, reminiscent of a disturbed ant's nest. The man-power, or should I say woman-power, certainly complimented the lack of sophisticated machinery. Men wielding large dutch hoe-like implements filled small metal bowls with sand. These were lifted onto the heads of carriers, mainly women, who formed a human chain. The small babies, lying on the mounds of sand, provided a welcome diversion for the mothers, as they periodically suckled them to quiet their cries.

Adjustment to this amazing Bombay life came little by little. Soon we were accepting crowds and noise as normal, but not enjoying them. There were times when we would close our door and long to be able to shut out everything of India and make a little England inside. On one such occasion as my heart turned to God my thoughts condemned me. I wrote to my sister Gwen, "Bombay is a dreadful place! Everything is riddled with corruption, life is so cheap, the poor and the weak are treated so badly, there is no courtesy in everyday life, even the animals are treated with terrible cruelty and no one seems to notice". But I concluded, "Gwen, I couldn't come home, because I know this is just where the Lord wants me and He gives marvelous peace."

The Lord had called us to India to serve Him and to love the people. I began to cry out to the Lord; I was desperate for a baptism of love. What had seemed a successful Christian life in England was now inadequate. I did not have the selfless love this life demanded. I cried, "Lord, pour out Your love into my heart." Romans 5:5 became my theme, as I constantly claimed, "The love of God is shed abroad in my heart by the Holy Spirit".

Alan had his own set of problems. At times he was so homesick that he longed to board the next boat for England. He had become disillusioned working in The Gospel Literature Press. He had thought that it would be all joy sharing with others in the work of the Lord; but on the contrary, he was confronted with undercurrents of self-will, frayed tempers, harassments and delicate situations which he would never have dreamed would exist among Christian workers. At first he thought, *"I will not get involved,"* but soon found to his own condemnation, that he was as irritable as others. With completely inadequate facilities he was trying to introduce scientific methods of color printing into the press. On every front it was a frustrating uphill task. Spiritually drained, we turned to the Lord. How important it was to make a deliberate effort to receive strength day by day.

Six months after we arrived in India there was still no tenant for The Elms and the finances ran out; the property was to be sold. As we were considering the painful decisions suddenly news arrived; we had received gifts and a tenant was ready to move in immediately. The mortgage was paid on time and all the bills were covered. We knew the Lord intended the home to be for missionary families but this tenant was a businessman, not what we had expected. We were very puzzled.

I wrote to my sister, "God has shown Himself to be in control. We had cast this burden on the Lord. He knew the mortgage was due by July 5th and we were waiting for Him to provide." Again I found myself saying, "God is never early, but He is never late. He sent all the money that was needed." I told my sister, "My faith is in the One who cannot fail, who cannot change His mind, who is no man's debtor and who guides us continually." I went on to say, "I found it harder to believe the house would go into debt, than to believe for its provision."

Through all these distressing circumstances the Lord was teaching us some in-depth lessons of faith. What do you do when you obey God and it does not work out as you expect? Waiting is so painful! But it is essential to maintain faith in the waiting time. We prayed and declared the Word; continually going back to the first instructions from the Lord. We trusted that somehow the Lord was working out His will though we couldn't see how. Eventually the Lord's plan came into place as mission families enjoyed long periods of time in our home and amazingly all the costs were continually covered.

Before the year was out, we had the great news that a missionary family from North India was to become our first missionary tenants in The Elms. The family, with their four children, was overjoyed at this provision and we were overjoyed at answered prayer. The Lord gave us grace to fight a prolonged fight of faith when nothing appeared to be happening, but eventually our faith was vindicated. From that time we never looked back; The Elms always had a missionary tenant. God provided financially and at the same time supplied a home for a family on furlough from the front lines. While this trial was playing out in England, in India all our needs were being met with more in reserve than we had ever had before! We were enjoying a period of plenty.

With the demands of the ministry that came upon both of us, I had to think through my responsibilities. It was the custom to leave children to the care of an *ayah*, but I was convinced that I should devote these valuable years to the children so that they became firmly established in the Lord. I was concerned for Rachel; she had had such huge upheavals in her young life and now she needed some stability, so I carefully limited my activities.

In December of our first year in Bombay, I wrote home, "God is wonderfully faithful in all His dealings with us, but it is a cause of great dismay that we are so utterly faithless in return. Truly God has supplied our every need in abundance and we have never lacked anything. Spiritually we find a surprising peace and calmness providing we stay very close to our Savior. If we allow anything to come between ourselves and Him, we succumb to the pressure of a thousand little material hardships and spiritual challenges that soon make us miserable and bad tempered. Then what use are we as a witness? This makes us realize afresh how helpless we are without the indwelling Spirit."

A fruitful work opened up for Alan among the teeming thousands of university students in the city. A small group of dedicated Christians was leading the work. Most of the students came from Hindu homes, though many of the young people were not as dedicated to the gods as their parents. Alan became a regular speaker at their retreats and camps and saw many saved and openly confess Christ. It was in these groups that Alan had his first regular opportunities to teach and preach. It became his 'on the job' training.

At the same time the Lord opened the door into a local hospital for me to minister to a nurses group. I had such joy leading many to Christ and then seeing them established in the church. Through these contacts one of the nurses took me to meet a patient, he was totally paralyzed below his upper chest region. Bishwanath Chowdhuri, a Brahmin Hindu was earnestly seeking Christ and reading the New Testament. Alan then faithfully visited him and had the joy of leading his first person to Christ in India. They became good friends; Alan was determined to make arrangements to bring him to church on Sundays despite Bishwanath's huge physical problems. Some months later the wonderful day arrived and Alan found the superhuman strength to carry this full grown man down into the water, to be baptized. It was a miracle that Alan in his own weak state accomplished such a feat.

John and Reta Hutchinson had taken the pastorate of the Baptist church where we attended. They had been in India for about eight years as Youth for Christ organizers from Canada. Their work had been hard and disappointing. Converts had been few and problems many. With four growing children they frequently found themselves with nowhere to live, like so many in Bombay. The Gospel they preached and believed to be all powerful somehow was not meeting the needs of their lives; with blighted hope they turned to the Lord seeking his fullness. Alan and I found a common bond with John and Reta in our one desire for a fruitful Christian life. Instinctively we knew the answer to our need was the Holy Spirit and our constant prayer was, "Lord fill us", and then we tried by various means to be 'filled'. First we concentrated upon more bible study, then more prayer, which ended up in struggling to get an unknown blessing from what seemed to be an unwilling God.

Before we had left England we had both sought an Acts 2 infilling of the Holy Spirit. One morning when Alan returned from an early prayer meeting, he told me that he had received the infilling of the Spirit by faith. After a few days nothing seemed changed and the faith of that morning evaporated till it was just a memory. At about the same period, one night God wakened me from my sleep; I left the warm bed and went down into the cold living room. Falling on my knees, I knew the Lord had called me there. I opened my Bible and waited. Only one thing was in my mind; I wanted to be filled with the Holy Spirit, although I didn't understand what that really meant or what to expect. My eyes fell on the words in Ezekiel 2:1-2, "The Spirit entered into me and set me upon my feet." I claimed those words for myself, thanking and rejoicing in Him. My heart was delighted as I read on through the whole chapter and on to the next. Thanking God I went back to bed. For the next few days the reality of God's presence remained with me and I rejoiced in His word. The Spirit had entered into me! But it was not long before the experience became a memory and I was again floundering and wondering how to be filled with the Holy Spirit.

John, our Pastor, preached out of the hunger and desire of his own heart and stressed the need of a definite infilling of the Holy Spirit. By this time my thinking had gone full circle. I was sure that we only received the Holy Spirit at regeneration and that there was nothing more for us after that. Walking in Him would result in fullness as we grew in maturity. I hardly dared to expect a definite experience of receiving the Holy Spirit in case I would again be disappointed. Soon, hunger for a greater depth of reality with God drove both of us again to seek the Lord in His Word. The desire to know the fullness of the Holy Spirit became a driving passion. This was fueled by avidly reading many testimonies and helpful books. We spent hours sharing our findings and encouraging each other in our search that continued into the next year.

CHAPTER 17

FIRST CLASS PAUPERS

Our first year in India was now behind us. Adjustments had been made, frustrations had been weathered and tribulation had worked patience (in some small measure). The hot season was again approaching and we began to think about a vacation out of Bombay. Financially it was impossible. After the plentiful supply of money when we first arrived, this second year had proved to be financially challenging; by living very simply we never lacked any essentials.

Alan had refused the offer of the very well paid job arranged for him by the chairman of the Kodak Company and then another that even provided a spacious flat and a good salary. We knew this wasn't God's way for us. The Lord had brought Alan to India so that he could give his time to Gospel Literature Service which did not pay any salary. We trusted that somehow the Lord would provide for us. Later, Alan did some part-time lecturing at the College of Printing which became a very effective door of opportunity to evangelize the students as well as providing some income.

The time to book vacation accommodation came and went. There was nothing we could do as we had no money. As we learned about the hill stations there was one place we really desired to go; Edgehill, a guest house in Landour, Mussoree, so we were delighted when we learned that Mrs. Norrish who managed Edgehill was in Bombay and wished to visit us. Soon we were talking about holidays. "I wish I had a room that I could offer you, I'm so sorry, as soon as one season ends people make their reservations for the next", said Mrs. Norrish. Later the same day we had a message. Mrs. Norrish had received mail with notice of a cancellation. "Look, she said, if you had asked me yesterday for a room I would have had to say, 'No'. And if tomorrow you had asked me, still I would have said 'no' because I had it in mind to offer the first cancellation to another family; but as it is today, I can say 'Yes'! I have a vacancy and it is for you!" she said, lovingly holding out the letter. Now we had a room, but still we had no money to travel!

The weeks fled by and our departure date drew near. The Lord chose this time to bring another testing into our lives. We were sure the Lord had supernaturally reserved our holiday accommodation for us, so with much stinting and saving we endeavored to prepare to go. When Alan returned home after another hot and busy day the uninteresting letter from the India Income Tax Department lay unopened on the side-board. Little did he know what a shock it contained. Casually, Alan pealed open the envelope, then read with stunned horror the huge tax demand and the accompanying threats to those who did not pay on time.

He made a quick calculation with his computer-type brain and out popped devastating information. Our carefully gathered vacation money would have to be used to pay the tax bill. A holiday was out of the question. Over the past few months our finances had dried up; we were even without money for our day to day living expenses.

During the following weeks we repeatedly turned over in our minds the guidance the Lord had given. We had seen His loving hand in the provision of the accommodation, the Lord was giving our family a vacation; we would all benefit from a change and respite from the heat. In spite of the fact that we had no money and that it was impossible to go, somehow we knew we would go to Edgehill. We were not behaving like ostriches and burying our heads in the sand; we squarely faced our impossible situation but preferred to believe the truth of God's Word to us.

The deadline came for buying the train tickets. We knew that if we left it another day the tickets would be sold out. That Saturday afternoon we prayed. Alan said, "Lord, do You want me to go and stand in line at the booking office even though I have no money? Do You want me to take such a step of faith?" We had read about Rees Howells who once did just that, then at the last moment someone stepped up and paid for his ticket. "Is that what I'm to do?" prayed Alan. We got up from our knees feeling sure that Alan was not to go to the station, but that the Lord had some other answer for us. The afternoon wore on and it seemed as if all hopes of buying tickets were lost.

Then the characteristic quick footsteps of Bill Thompson marched up to our front door. Alan was there at once in response to the loud ringing. Bill walked in with all the excitement of a small child and sat himself down on the edge of a chair. Bill opened up his bulging brief case, produced an envelope and presented it to Alan; in his hands he held first class round trip tickets for the whole journey to the north of India; Alan was speechless. We never dreamt that Bill would be our savior. He was very concerned for us and acutely aware of Alan's weak condition from continual bleeding; Bill understood our need to escape from the heat for a while. What thanksgiving filled the house! God had heard our prayer and our faith had been vindicated.

There were still ten days before we were due to leave but we still had very little money for the day to day expenses. God's word to us said, "Go". He re-emphasized it by giving us the tickets, but strangely not enough money for other expenses. For days I had been concocting meals from all sorts of scraps left in the bottom of jars and near empty storage tins. Somehow we managed to have something to eat each meal time and gave thanks heartily for whatever was set before us. I tried to find any food we could carry with us for the journey. The last remaining two eggs were hard boiled and together with one tin of baby food we took our cases laden with warm clothes to the station. Travel day had arrived! We were to embark upon our first long distance train journey which in India is an experience in itself. We would be two nights on trains besides many miles of road travel.

We had hoped to have money for the journey; for months no gift had come. The Printing College owed Alan money, but when he went to collect his salary they said, "Sorry, its holiday time. Come next week, perhaps your check will be ready then." This had gone on for weeks. Knowing that the Lord is in control of all things and that He will make even wrong things work together for good to those who love Him, we kept our hearts focused upon the Lord. We knew He was in charge of all our avenues of finance; we had not just hit an unfortunate set of coincidences, the Lord had prepared a trial of our faith. He had given us

His word and then it seemed as if He had withheld the finance to do His will.

A group of friends came to the railway station to see us off in good Indian style. Hopefully, I wondered if one of them would be prompted by the Lord to give us some money or some food. We settled ourselves in the compartment. The children were so excited, jumping around and getting themselves dirty. Soon the train started to draw slowly out of the station. I grabbed a large bag of popcorn that a friend pushed through the window. My heart shouted, "Thank You Jesus!" I gave the children a ration each and carefully guarded the rest. We settled back, counted our remaining few coins and realized that we had not enough even for food on the journey. We prayed and slept knowing that somehow the Lord would take care of us. In any case, someone was meeting us in Delhi.

The compartment door opened abruptly, "Dinner, Sir?" asked the steward.

"No, thank you." Alan replied.

"What about morning tea? Breakfast?"

"No, thank you." With a slam, the door was shut. Every meal the same episode was re-enacted.

The leisurely pace of Indian life had certainly infected the railways. Although we were on the fast mail train it stopped for quite long periods at all manner of stations. Some were classified as 'meal stops', where it was even possible to leave the train and eat a canteen type meal in a restaurant. If you preferred to remain in the compartment, the same food was served wrapped up in a banana leaf or on a large metal dish called a *thali*.

For those who couldn't go to the expense of a full meal there were a huge variety of snacks. Every few moments a different face would appear at the barred window shouting his wares.

"Iess cream! Iess cream!" (Ice cream! Ice cream!)

"Chay! chay! garam chay!"

"Sandweech! Sandweech!"

"Chicki! Chicki!"

"Garam dhood, garam dhood!" The cacophony of noise was fascinating.

Coolies, wearing brightly colored turbans balancing an incredible amount of baggage on their heads wove their way in and out of the crowds of people sitting about on the platforms. Some looked as if they had been there for days with their bedding rolled out to serve as a table cloth as they ate their food. Others were stretched out fast asleep despite the din. A man standing under a water tap was having a bath, wearing nothing but a small loin cloth; he was thoroughly lathered from head to foot and enjoying the cool water. Bathing in such a public place didn't appear to cause him the least embarrassment.

Beggars would silently stand with an extended hand and fix you with a stare that would make you wilt; then there were those promising blessings from the gods if only you would give a few *naya paise*. The blessings soon turned to cursing if you didn't oblige. Beggars, beggars everywhere! The blind, the lepers, the devil possessed, the maniacs, the drunkards and the cripples; as soon as the train stopped they would spy our foreign faces and descend on us in droves. Some were happy to sing for a few coins, others displayed their deformed limbs. The most heart rending sight were the beggar children; draped in filthy bits of rag with their unkempt hair mated with years of dirt. They moved around in gangs and would fight with each other to get our attention. If money was given to the smaller children, the big ones would move in with bully tactics and snatch it from them.

Never before had I been confronted with dire poverty at such close quarters. It repulsed me. I grappled with my churned up emotions. I found their persistent demands irritating although I knew I should not. It was another chance for the Lord to show me the poverty of my own heart. They were people but they didn't seem like people. I hated the devil for bringing them down so low.

During the middle of the following day the sides of the train were too hot to touch, as it slowly chugged along. The fan whirled noisily stirring up the hot air as we tried to sleep on our berths, the warm drinking water did little to quench our insatiable thirst.

The shouts and calls of the *wallas* selling their wares greeted us as the train drew into Delhi. Here we were to change trains. Coolies jumped up into the compartments looking for the most affluent passengers and sizing up their luggage. Decisions made in those few split seconds decided their daily income. We were craning our necks out of the compartment window looking expectantly for a young man who had been sent to help us to negotiate our way safely to the next train that would take us on to Dehra Dun. It was not too difficult to pick out a Christian face from the crowd, soon greetings were over and the young man left us in a hurry to be off to another appointment. With him, as far as we could see, went our last chance of help. We had hoped and prayed that he would have some money for us. We were hungry.

Recriminations began to rise in our hearts. *"Surely Lord, You have failed us."* We collected our things together and Alan prepared to move our heavy trunk to the other platform to await the night train. Alan could not lift the trunk alone, so our last few *paise* were spent on the coolie. We sat on our luggage in a dejected state. The children were tired with traveling. We were all very hot and dirty. The good smell from the *bhelpuri* stalls wafted over to us and our gastric juices did overtime. We all wanted a good meal and a drink. The children finished off the popcorn.

We drank the remaining water; its earthy plastic taste was unpleasant. We were both deep in thought. The children had been so contented on the journey and had not asked for a thing, but temptation arrived as the ice cream man pushed his cart past us, followed by a Coca-Cola stall inching its way along and stopping just a few yards away. We all watched as a small knot of people stood around sucking deeply at their straws.

A tall European walking along the platform in a businesslike fashion caught our attention. At the same moment he noticed us and coming across asked where we were going and what reservations we had. Once introductions were made, Alan realized he had met the man before in Bombay. He worked in the Inter-Missions Business Office. He suggested that as there were a number of missionaries travelling on the same night train, we should get our reservations changed, so that we could all be together in nearby compartments. By this time we were just so thankful for anyone who could help us. We felt mentally, physically and spiritually exhausted.

In expert fashion he arranged for our luggage to be moved and like a fussy mother hen settled us with his party for the second night's journey. Next morning we awoke early. There was a thrill in my heart as I looked out on the beautiful countryside and smelt the freshness of the cool breeze coming from the Himalayas, 'the roof of the world'. I thought how privileged we were to be going to such a place. *"Today we will be there. Thank You Lord."* Then my mind wandered, soon we would be leaving the train and again we would need money. We could not manage without a coolie. I guess I was worrying. Tea was served, how good it tasted! We drank thankfully and ate sandwiches that were offered followed by all kinds of snacks, the children were happy.

Using his last scrap of energy Alan strapped up our bedding roll and hoisted it towards the door. Our efficient mother hen (or perhaps we should have called him our guardian angel) said he would call coolies to carry the baggage of the whole party. He then went to negotiate for a vehicle to drive us the last twenty-two miles to Mussoorie. We had had no idea that still there lay such a distance ahead of us. It was now pointless trying to be independent. So thankfully we submitted to being organized as one of the party, though constantly aware that we had no money to meet any of the expenses.

Both of us were having a continual conversation with the Lord. *"Why have You not provided? Lord You have failed us."* Depression and anxiety are very tiring and as we clambered into the jeep, exhaustion took over. It was a bumpy ride, up and up the mountain. Occasionally I would take in a sweep of the exhilarating view as we lurched around a bend and then I would doze again.

We collected the children and our belongings together and got down from the jeep. Soon the party was besieged by coolies all shouting and talking at once. We couldn't understand a word any of them said, but again our guardian angel was there quietly organizing everything. Taking one look at us he said, "You will not make it on foot, you had better get into this rickshaw." The hill was very steep. We sat in the precarious vehicle feeling horribly embarrassed as two men positioned like horses pulled us up the hill. In front of us was our large blue trunk strapped on the back of a small man who steadily climbed the one in four gradient like a mountain goat. We were now on our own; the rest of the party had gone in different directions. We had said profuse thank you's to our guardian angel as he waved us goodbye.

Slowly we were dragged up through the bazaar and on to Edgehill. I mused, *"Here we are traveling like rajas in a rickshaw, but we have no money not even to pay the coolies at the other end. Lord this is crazy! It's good to know that You are in charge and that somehow you have all this ridiculous situation under control."* Such was my desperate conversation with the Lord. *"Perhaps there will be mail awaiting us,"* I thought.

We were glad to get down from the rickshaw as it pulled up in front of the attractive property. Mrs. Norrish ran out to greet us, "Don't pay those coolies, she called, I will settle with them. I know the rates, just come inside, tea and toast are waiting here for you." Again we were rescued from another difficult situation; we sank into the basket chairs and drank what seemed to be the most delicious tea. We had arrived. Our hearts overflowed in thankfulness and a sense of relief that at least for the coming few weeks, a bed and food was provided and we had no immediate need for money; except to pay our debts. We encouraged ourselves with the thought that by the time we were due to leave, God would provide.

CHAPTER 18

THE SCHOOL OF FAITH

We woke the next morning rested and looking forward to the day. After the suffocating heat of Bombay it was wonderful to smell the crisp, clear air. For a moment it was a beautiful diversion, but it did not take long for reality to hit home. Still hanging over our heads was the painful question, how can we repay Mrs. Norrish for the rickshaw coolies and our share of the expenses incurred on the journey? Alan decided to apologize to Mrs. Norrish and tell her that we intended to repay the money as soon as some came. The whole situation was very humiliating. Our thoughts went round in circles, nothing made sense. We just could not understand why the Lord had not provided the money for us.

Alan went into the office and asked Mrs. Norrish if any mail had come for us "No, but let me loan you fifty rupees" was her immediate response. Alan declined the offer and said he would prefer to wait to see what the Lord would do. We had never borrowed money as we firmly believed, and lived by the principle, that God knew our needs and would provide. In a previous time of trial, I had coined the phrase "If it is God's will, it is God's bill!" To us, borrowing money in a trial was tantamount to helping ourselves out of the problem, rather than honoring God and waiting for His answer. Waiting is part of trusting in God and perhaps the hardest thing to do. We can always end a financial trial by delivering ourselves with a loan. For us to borrow money in that kind of situation would have seemed to demonstrate our failure to trust God. Similarly, credit cards may bring relief in many a difficult situation, but to resort to them would block the way to a miracle and hinder the building of faith. These attitudes towards faith grew in us through the discipling we received from the Elliott's and the steady diet of challenging biographies of the people of faith we had read. We recognized that those who did great exploits for God were always great believers. They had to have a

God who was bigger than any circumstance and who they knew would never fail them. We would declare, "Abraham's God is our God, Hudson Taylor's God is our God, and what He did for C.T. Studd He will do for us." Here we were again having our faith stretched. When we emerged from this trial, our declarations would have a clearer ring of reality.

The next day Mrs. Norrish called Alan into the office. "Come and sit down. A guest has just settled their account and gave this for anyone in the house in financial need, so take it from the Lord. This is for you." She handed him an envelope; inside were fifty rupees. Instead of borrowing fifty rupees now we owned fifty rupees! What a confirmation. We were right to wait for the Lord. Delighted by this token of our Father's loving care, we praised and thanked Him.

It was a great weight off Alan's mind to pay off the various small sums we owed. As he returned from visiting our guardian angel he purchased a tube of toothpaste and some Indian letter forms. The toothpaste was a luxury we had not had for many weeks and the letter forms seemed essential; with long days ahead of us and piles of unanswered correspondence we could use our days to write. The fifty rupees was gone and we were penniless again but the lunch bell would ring, good food would be on the table and we had no bill to pay till the end of the month; we were not going to worry.

Whilst Alan was gone I sat alone in the sun reveling in the view, enjoying the birds and the scent of hundreds of exotic flowers wafting on the breeze. Flamboyant butterflies showing off fabulous colors flitted between the flowers. If I had had a little more energy I would have been chasing them around to get a better view. For me to see one of God's creations for the very first time, is an important event in my life and always fills me with awe. Once I was examining an unusual brilliant insect scurrying in the grass and I asked Salome, who was sitting with me, what it was. I never forgot her answer, "Oh that's just one of God's millions!" God's millions could keep me enthralled for the rest of my days!

The view created a peace that I could almost taste. Sitting in the comfortable garden chair, I fixed my gaze way beyond the distant haze. It was as if I was looking directly into the face of the Lord. I was mulling over in my mind all the painful days, even weeks of trial that we were still going through. We were living on crumbs from the Master's table and there seemed to be no end in sight. In anguish again I said, "Lord You have failed me, You said You would provide" and pointing to my Bible I said, "I could fault You; You have not kept Your word. You gave me promises but You have failed me!" My words fell into the silence. All was quiet. Deep down in the depths of my spirit, something incomprehensible churned around and then welled up. With tears streaming down my face, I blurted out, "My God but I still trust You, I cannot but trust You!" The awesome Spirit of the Lord came down over me. I knew I would follow Him anywhere, whatever the conditions; something deep within me could not, not trust Him.

I discovered that there is a very close union between intimacy with the Father and faith. It seems as if the persistent pressing in to have the object of our faith, flings doors of access into the knowledge of God wide open. We come to know Him in ways perhaps not possible by any other means. Victories of faith secure far more than the object of our faith. I found that in an imperceptible manner my heart was drawn into an ever deeper knowing of God who was my Provider and then, in that knowledge, I saw myself and my motives more clearly. Truly, "As we behold Him we are being changed from one degree of glory to another."

Having time to sit and feast my eyes and heart on the glorious view also provided the right atmosphere to hear God and so be drawn into a deeper knowing of God. I came to understand that the strength of my trust dictates the depth of my relationship. The very trial of faith drives us into God and awakens deep, otherwise inaccessible areas of our being. Once awakened to enjoy this kind of fellowship, even if it is the fellowship of His sufferings, the quickened love is never satisfied with less.

Gently over the following days the Lord showed us how proud we were. He said, "I provided for you through other people, was that not good enough?" We had to admit, He had provided, but we didn't like that kind of provision. We had felt humiliated. Slowly we accepted that He has the right to provide for us in whatever manner He chooses. Little by little the Lord was chipping away at our proud, self-righteous ways.

The glorious days flowed lazily one into another. The children were happy enough playing in the dirt and swinging on the swings. Duncan, just one year old, with great determination learned to walk getting up from countless falls on the rough stony paths. Perhaps that was prophetic for Duncan; he first walked on mountain slopes.

For Alan there were a new set of difficulties, we had not realized the altitude would have an adverse effect upon him. He found breathing difficult so our activities were curtailed to sitting in the garden, or at the most, taking a gentle wander along a fairly level path. There was plenty of time to talk, to think and to read.

A gentle shower at night had caused the heat haze over the plains to vanish. We sat in the inviting garden chairs gazing at the panoramic view. The beauty all about us had a relaxing effect. Like a butterfly, my eyes flitted from flower to flower, from tree to mossy bank, from pattern of shade to sunlight and on to busy garden insects. In those moments some deep starved part of my being was quickened. Then my eyes returned to drink deeply at each individual beauty, like a bee finding satisfaction in the sweetness hidden in each blossom.

Bombay's congested streets devoid of such beauty had been my home for fifteen months. There, no butterflies venture or bees find satisfaction. There the trees didn't glisten with morning dew, but their leaves, heavy with factory grime, cried out for the next monsoon, waiting for their annual wash.

Daisy, a missionary from Pakistan, looked up from her letter writing. She was happy to put her correspondence aside for a while as we drank morning coffee together. Drawing her chair alongside mine she began to say how encouraged she had felt listening to Alan and myself give our testimonies in the fellowship gathering the evening before.

Little did she know that when I left the meeting to return to our room, I felt anything but encouraged. I lay on my bed staring into the darkness talking with the Lord a long time before sleep overtook me. It was true, I had a testimony to tell of the wonderful things that the Lord had done, but now I felt dry and empty. I longed for an up to date testimony. I wanted to experience the 'now' blessing and presence of God.

As I told Daisy the thoughts of my heart, I found a sympathetic listener. Then, I became the listener as she told me, that because of sickness, she had spent some prolonged periods in Landour and during this imposed rest, God had blessed her. Three years previously she had heard the ministry of the Rev. David McKee, an Irish Presbyterian missionary. This led her to experience the baptism of the Holy Spirit. I was not used to that expression but was interested to know what it meant in her experience, especially if the reality of the experience had remained with her or vanished like the morning mist. She assured me that she was still living in the fruits of the blessing received three years previously.

I told her of my struggles and how I found living in India had so painfully exposed the poverty of my Christian life. I longed to overcome in every situation as the Word clearly told me I should, but too often the situation overcame me! I shared my hunger to be filled with the Holy Spirit. I had claimed it many times but it seemed I was like a proverbial leaky bucket; whatever I received soon drained away.

Daisy spoke to my heart. I hung on her every word. I couldn't hear enough. Hope and expectation rose in me; perhaps now I would find that 'something' for which I yearned. I told Alan of my conversations and then we both avidly read the magazine Daisy had lent us. It was one of the many publications produced by the new Charismatic movement sweeping the USA and the UK in the mid-sixties. There were stories of people from all walks of life who for various reasons had sought the baptism of the Holy Spirit. They testified that through this experience they found power to meet their individual needs and were then able to live a godly and solid Christian witness.

Browsing through the library books in the guest house we discovered answers to more of our questions. Each added item of information was like a building block bringing clarity to the major question, "How can I be filled with the Holy Spirit?" Much of our time was spent in bible study and reading. In between pushing Rachel on the swing and grabbing Duncan before he fell on his face, we tried to discuss our gleanings.

Alan said, "In each testimony that I have read, the person was prayed for with the laying on of hands."

I added, "But what of the man we read about yesterday who was baptized in the Spirit as he lay in his bathtub!?"

"If I remember correctly, he previously had had hands laid upon him", Alan replied. "It seems that when he relaxed in the warm water he stopped trying to 'get' the baptism but just thanked and worshipped God for who He is, and the Lord met him. Perhaps all that time the Lord was waiting to pour out His Spirit upon him, but he was too frustrated in trying to receive. What do you think about tongues?"

"I wish I really knew what it meant. Each person that I have read about spoke in tongues and I know Daisy does. Perhaps we will never understand till we receive," I said, and so the talk went on.

On the mountainside, sheltered among the tall trees, was a small wooden hut. It provided the perfect place of retreat for those who wished to pray. Once the children were sleeping in their beds we closed the door softly and went to keep our appointment with Daisy. She hadn't been surprised when we asked if she would pray for us. She said, "The Lord told me you would ask and He said I was to say 'yes'."

We walked along the narrow path in single file, each of us deep in our own thoughts. Only the moonlight lit our way. The springy humus under our feet was freshly wetted by evening dew. Pushing open the heavy door we entered the sparsely furnished room. Dropping to our knees, we began to pray with great expectancy. "Lord You know our need. We are asking You now according to Your promise, give us the Holy Spirit. Lord, we are asking, come and fill us now!" Daisy laid her hands upon us and prayed softly in what I assumed was tongues. The sweet presence of Jesus was so real.

Suddenly, without warning a strong wind swept through the trees outside. They swayed and groaned under the impact of the powerful blast. The wind seemed fraught with meaning. I thought of the upper room and the mighty rushing wind; surely the Holy Spirit is here. The atmosphere felt pregnant; the wind in the trees seemed to be a wind in the room. In eager anticipation we waited for the Spirit to come upon us. I don't know what experience we were expecting, but with bated breath we waited and waited. No one wanted to be the first to move from their knees; it would seem like admitting failure. We had followed steps that we thought the Bible taught, we had asked for the Holy Spirit. Daisy had laid her hands upon us; we had expected to receive but nothing, it seemed, had happened.

When we returned to our room we knelt by the bed and tried to speak in tongues. I thought that sounds would come and somehow my tongue would speak by itself. But my efforts only added to my frustration which was directed towards God. I knew that He had been very near to us in the prayer hut and had somehow been in the wind. In my frustration I said, "Lord God, You moved everything, but You didn't move me."

The next morning my mind took up where it had left off the night before. Round and round went the questions and reasoning's. *"Why hadn't the Lord come and baptized us in the Spirit? We had sought him exactly the way that He led us."* We had a short period while the children had their afternoon rest, when I knew I could have some uninterrupted time with the Lord. As soon as the children were sleeping I took my Bible and found a quiet place in the sitting room. I wanted the Lord to speak to me so badly; I needed the Lord to speak to me. Opening my Bible at John's Gospel chapter 14, I began to read. The words spoke so powerfully to my thirsty heart that leapt with anticipation as I read, "I will not leave you desolate, I will come to you." I rejoiced in the words. My eyes lingered over each phrase, and then I lovingly savored verse 21, "And he shall manifest himself to you." I sat in the bulky armchair praising God. "Jesus, You are not going to leave me desolate; You are going to come to me. You will manifest Yourself to me. Oh Thank You! Thank You Jesus." Strangely it did not seem that I was reading the words off the page but that they were being personally dropped from the Father's hand upon me. The words were alive.

I said, "Lord, I don't want to hope that You have manifested Yourself to me. I don't want to 'take it by faith'. I want to know that You have done it. You said, You would manifest Yourself to me. Lord Jesus, I am waiting." I sat with my hands outstretched, I believed that something wonderful was about to happen. I didn't know what to expect when Jesus manifested Himself, but I knew that I would know about it. My hands were upturned and cupped, picturing my heart that was reaching out for overflowing fullness. Jesus will manifest Himself; Jesus will come to me.

The Lord spoke quietly to my heart, "It is done." His word sank into me. Although it seemed like a paradox, I knew from that moment that the baptism of the Holy Spirit was given to me and yet my upraised hands spoke of my desire for experience.

A small instance that Daisy had recounted flashed into my mind. A lady in her home church in Canada had been prayed for to receive the baptism of the Holy Spirit. Nothing visible happened, yet this woman believed. Each day, after seeing her husband off to work, she would go to her room and thank God for giving her the baptism of the Spirit. This went on day after day, then month after month, until one morning, six months later in just the same way, she bade her husband goodbye and went into her bedroom. Again, she lifted up her voice and thanked the Lord for His good gift of the Spirit to her. Before she knew what had happened the Spirit fell upon her in power, she was engulfed in the supernatural presence of God and praised Him in tongues.

Quietly and with determination I said to the Lord, "Even if I have to say thank you as a declaration of faith for the next six months, I will, because I know in heaven the transaction is done. Jesus will manifest Himself to me!" Abruptly I was interrupted, the tea bell was ringing and the children's afternoon rest was at an end. But it did not matter. The issue was settled; the Lord had said all that was needed.

Alan remained unwell, breathless and bleeding throughout the holiday, so we contented ourselves with sitting, admiring the view, reading and fellowshipping with many fine Christians. Endlessly finding occupations for our two children became the most energetic activity of the day.

Although we had seen our Father provide exactly for our needs on many occasions, as the date of our departure drew near, anxieties crept in. When the mail arrived, we looked hopefully in our pigeon hole. We didn't want to face another journey like the first epic one. The Lord knew we were weary of the situation but He longed to bring us to a place of unquestioning trust. So He kept us in his school of faith and said nothing! We were to learn at a new depth that He was completely in control of everything. We need never to have worried.

As the day came for us to return to Bombay, anonymous gifts appeared in our bedroom. When we received our bill, miraculously we had sufficient funds to pay because miracles happened daily! In the same miraculous ways as we left to catch the train, enough money for the journey and some to spare was pressed into our hands. The Lord delighted to provide for us in a variety of ways, even through people totally unknown to us. He wanted us to grasp once and for all that it was He alone who controlled our finances; wherever we were and whatever the need, great or small, He knew about it and would provide.

Once back in Bombay, we anticipated our difficulties would end. The long overdue check from the Printing College was sure to be awaiting collection. Alan returned crestfallen from a fruitless visit to the College Office. The Treasurers Department had failed to apply for his salary. Now it had to be considered in the new financial year and would probably take two months before it materialized! Obviously the Lord intended to keep us in His school of faith.

Thanks were given with unusual fervor for whatever was set on the table. The days passed slowly as we waited for some respite while it seemed again as if the Lord was quite unconcerned on our behalf; but unknown to us, He was preparing a perfect deliverance.

A commanding ring at the front door announced Bill Thompson looking as usual, rather pleased with himself. He sat down and wasting no time said, "We have just finished the trustees meeting. I came straight round to you because it was agreed we should give you this," he said, handing Alan a check.

"Wow! Where did this come from?" said Alan astonished.

"Well it's a long story, but listen. Some months ago a young couple in Finland was converted to Christ. They really meant business with God, yielding their lives and all they possessed to the Lord. When He told them to sell their car and give the funds to missions, they obeyed. This gift Bill said, taking the check in his hand, represents the proceeds from that sale. We received it with a covering letter saying that it was for the personal use of someone on the GLS staff. The Trustees unanimously agreed that it was for you." Words seemed inadequate and soon turned into praise. How lovingly the Lord met our need. Again we felt humbled receiving the generosity of unknown saints.

The generous hearts of the donors and their gift became the key that opened the Lord's storehouse to us. The next day, the Income Tax Department returned the large sum of money they had demanded a few months previously; apparently a mistake had been made. Then, with no explanation the Printing College produced Alan's long delayed salary check. The painful delay in paying Alan's salary and the frightening mistake of the Indian Tax Department were used by the Lord as instructors in the school of faith. After five very lean, painful months we suddenly possessed more than we had ever had since being in India.

Many years later we realized that trials are the means by which the Lord builds faith and trains us in faith. It is painful to develop strong physical muscles and requires persistence even when it hurts, in the same way faith is built by pushing through, staying determined and not turning back, regardless of the present pain. As we graduate from each level in this continuing school of faith the goal is that every action, belief and decision should reflect deeply rooted trust in God; this is unshakable faith.

CHAPTER 19

HEAVENLY PLACES

We sat in the back of the Hutchinson's big old American car. The sudden monsoon deluge made the night black hiding all our faces as we attempted to tell John and Reta of our time in Landour. Our conversation had a slight awkwardness as we were not sure how they would react to the question of the baptism in the Holy Spirit.

John had also decided that this was a good opportunity to tell us of their holiday in the South of India. Likewise they were wondering how we would react if they mentioned the baptism in the Holy Spirit. So there in the dark we gently probed each other. John continued the disjointed conversation as he mentioned Rev. David McKee, who we remembered had been instrumental in bringing blessing into Daisy's life. We realized that while at opposite ends of the country, we had both had similar spiritual experiences. Then caution was thrown to the wind and with enthusiasm we shared our stories, laughing and praising God for the way in which He had led us individually and yet we had both come to the same conclusions. We were of one heart and mind, longing to see the full manifestation of the power of God in our lives through the baptism in the Holy Spirit.

John introduced revival prayer meetings in the church. Now looking back, perhaps a better name would have been 'Struggle Meetings'! We gathered with expectancy, crying to God to bless us and to revive the church. We knew so little about praising and rejoicing, rather it seemed as if we were trying to squeeze a blessing out of the hand of a reluctant God. Regardless, our merciful Father was answering our prayers.

The church began to prosper, numbers increased and spiritual hunger was evident. As we considered how we should move forward as a church, it seemed right to invite the Rev. David McKee. We were confident that he could lead us all to experience the power of the Spirit. Unfortunately his calendar was full and he was not accepting any further engagements. This was a disappointment, but despite the initial setback both John and Alan believed he would eventually come so we continued to pray.

When we learned that David McKee was to be the speaker at meetings in a city about 125 miles from Bombay, it took no time for both the Hutchinsons and ourselves to rearrange appointments and go. David preached powerfully from Romans chapter six, about knowing ourselves dead to sin and alive unto God. Interestingly, John Hutchinson had been going through the same passage during our weekly Bible studies. These had deeply challenged me but at the same time I was frustrated. One day I said, "Lord I have tried to be dead to myself till I'm 'blue in the face', but all I discover is that I am very much alive!"

David McKee told a story of a preacher who dug a hole in the garden. He then invited his congregation to come and bury their old selves by faith. He stressed our need to believe the Bible and not our feelings. God was speaking to the depths of my being. It is one thing to have faith for finance, but now, I needed a revelation of how to have faith for victory over sin. I wanted unshakable faith to know myself dead to sin and alive unto God. The words at the end of Matthew 5, "Be perfect therefore as your Father in Heaven is perfect" always troubled me. How can I live this kind of life?

Sitting on the back of Alan's motorbike, going home after the meeting, I was pondering all these things. Suddenly the truth became reality as it hit my heart. I believed the Word. Right there on the back of the motorbike I said, "I know I died with Christ and now I live with Him. Lord, I believe; I reckon myself dead, really dead to sin and alive unto God. Sin shall not have dominion over me. I praise You Lord!" Then by faith, I threw my old self over the hedge somewhere between Deolali and Nasik! It was done and I was rejoicing. I didn't need to understand; I knew and I believed.

I didn't seem to be any different the next day; I hadn't suddenly turned into a sinless saint! If I had wanted to doubt, I had plenty of opportunity.

The Lord led me to understand that by deciding to believe God's word, He had begun a process in me. Over the following weeks and months He began to work the truth into the fabric of my life just as I had believed.

John was beaming as he walked down the steps of the church towards us; he had heard the characteristic sound of Alan's two stroke motor bike come into the compound. "Praise the Lord, Alan I was waiting for you. Look, I've had a letter from David McKee. He has agreed to come for a 'Week to Seek God'." As the week approached there was a joyful anticipation among the hungry ones. We sensed it would be a crisis week in our spiritual lives and we were prepared for anything.

CHAPTER 20

THE WEEK TO SEEK GOD

It was April 1965 when David McKee arrived and the meetings began with much anticipation. Present at one of the morning prayer sessions was an elderly gentleman, a visitor off a passing ship. During a time for open sharing he said, "In my experience over many years I have found that God does not keep anyone waiting for the baptism of the Holy Spirit. If there should be a delay in receiving, the fault is their own and not God's." His sweeping statement didn't receive much attention and I guess was soon forgotten by most.

Over lunch that day, Alan and I discussed his remark. We had both reacted strongly. Alan had thought, "He has made a mistake here. I'm not keeping God waiting, I have sought Him wholeheartedly." My thoughts were much the same. I was convinced that we were waiting for a sovereign intervention from God. I found it hard to agree with the visitor that there was still something in me that was preventing the glorious answer to my prayer. However it disturbed me. I had been faithfully declaring and thanking the Lord that the baptism in the Holy Spirit was mine. Was this the time when Jesus would 'manifest Himself to me' and 'not leave me desolate' as He had promised? Many times I reminded the Lord that I expected to experience His manifestation and not just 'take it by faith'! Over the months the Lord had drawn my heart out after Himself so that I asked Him, "Turn over every stone in my life, get to the bottom of me!" I had met some people who spoke in tongues, but their lives did not have the fragrance of God. I said, "Lord, I don't just want a gift of tongues or an experience, I want You."

One day the words I was quietly reading stung my heart, "If you have a besetting sin it's because you love it!" My eyes were riveted upon the words. I read them again and again; it was as if God was directly speaking to me. Recently the Lord had been showing me my critical, sarcastic tongue. He applied these words right where it hurt! Why didn't I want to receive the truth? I quickly sprang to my own defense, "But I don't love it Lord. You know how often I've prayed about it and how often I've asked for forgiveness." The Lord repeated the same words in my heart, "It's because you love it." Suddenly my sarcasm had become huge; it seemed to block my way to God.

As I thought over the Lord's words I realized I derived a secret pleasure from being cleverly sarcastic. Slowly I admitted, "Yes Lord, you are right, I do love it." Then I wept. The guilt lay heavy upon me and there seemed no immediate way of escape.

We arrived early at the church for the evening meeting. The late sunshine flooded though the doorway as a small group of people tried to get past those talking. Everyone wanted front seats! The church was filled with an unusual company of people; those hungry for the word, hungry for the power of the Holy Spirit; and those ready to abandon everything to just have more of the Lord.

For me it was a time of the most intense seeking after God. The desire for Him consumed me so that it was as if no other person existed; not even Alan, who was there next to me but pursuing his own unique search. The only intimacy I desired was with the Lord.

I was captured by every hymn and impacted by preaching that pierced deeper than I had known before. The meeting drew to a close. Everything within me had to respond to the Lord. I privately confessed my sins of sarcasm and lack of love asking the Lord to work a miracle. I longed to be an altogether different person. I was still struggling with my failure to consistently live a Christ exalting Christian life but I would not forsake my stand of faith, "I was dead to sin and alive unto God!" I was quite unaware of any one else; my attention was locked into the One alone who could meet my need.

While singing that glorious hymn, "Jesus I am resting, resting in the joy of what Thou art", something wonderful happened. I knew, with the same assurance that I had experienced almost a year before in the sitting room of Edgehill, the baptism in the Holy Spirit was mine. I rested in His word and felt secure, but paradoxically said, "Lord, I am waiting; come now and manifest Yourself to me." In those few moments the Lord was so precious to me, that if I were never to experience anything more of the Lord He was then worthy of all my praise for all eternity.

Evening by evening I responded to the Lord, walking to the front of the church declaring my need, with no care for what others thought. The final meeting arrived; again the church was filled with hungry people long before the meeting time. The atmosphere was bathed in prayer and with a great sense of expectancy. I sat next to a missionary friend who had traveled 200 miles to be present, she was longing for the Holy Spirit's power; then the church secretary and his wife took the remaining places in the row and the opening hymn was announced.

My heart was so tender toward God and leapt to respond as the closing invitation was given. People all over the church stood, my missionary friend was one of the first to her feet. Suddenly I was very aware of the secretary's wife next to me; I so wanted to stand but felt foolish. I wondered what she would think, I was supposed to be a missionary and a leader but each evening I was standing before the Lord and publically admitting my need. The tussle only lasted a moment. *"Lord do You really want me to stand again?"* There was no need to wait for a response, I knew what to do. I stood quietly and said to the Lord, "This is the last meeting. I'm waiting, I'm waiting, please come to me!" I did not want to leave that hallowed place.

An open invitation was given to a prayer meeting in the Pastor's home upstairs. Though it was late, the hungry ones trudged up the steep spiral steps in single file. Chairs of all shapes and sizes were hurriedly arranged down the sides of the very long room and about sixty people seated themselves with unusual eagerness for a prayer meeting. Timid folk took places where they were obscured. The most comfortable seats were left to the last. No one wanted to appear eager for his own welfare. The room was hushed in a quiet embarrassment as the Holy Spirit continued his powerful work of exposure of people's hearts. We wondered what was going to happen next. Our ignorance didn't matter for God already knew what He would do.

David's hoarse authoritative voice rang out, "Rend your hearts and not your garments!" Alan and I were both startled by the word; it came with power directly into our hearts. Alan was visibly impacted while trying to keep his composure. Weeping broke the pregnant silence and then, one after another people prayed, making deep confessions of sin. The private exposure now became public, the one thing we all secretly feared. In His determination to cleanse us, God was at work forcing out confessions such as would normally be reserved for the death bed. The moments of sublime intimacy I had enjoyed an hour before were gone in this very different presence of God.

I felt compelled to bring into the open my sin of criticism and sarcasm. Suddenly the weight of it was intolerable. Crying, I blurted it all out before the Lord. His response was wonderful. The heavy weight of guilt had gone. Sitting on the edge of my chair I praised God, I knew at last my sin was gone, I was free and forgiven. At the same time many things were happening all about me. The room was alive with Holy Spirit activity; problems and bondages were banished, hearts were being set free and weeping gave place to joy. A young Indian Youth for Christ worker was so overjoyed that he stood up with his hands raised directly above his head. He looked as if he was about to jump straight into heaven! He stretched out his long skinny body as high as he could with his face glowing with joy. Nothing could keep him quiet as he shouted his praises.

For a long time John, Reta, Alan and I had been praying for deacons who were full of faith and full of the Holy Spirit. So imagine our delight when in the middle of a flow of Holy Spirit repentance, that had been mixed with effervescent joy, one of the deacons sitting on the opposite side of the room began to pray with wracking sobs as he sought to get right with God. His wife whispered, "Rev. McKee please pray for him. He needs healing, he has a hernia." But we knew his needs were much deeper. Everyone was in prayer as John and David laid hands upon Mr. Sarthe's head. I thanked God for bringing him to repentance and pleaded with the Lord to pour out His Spirit upon this broken man. Sitting on the opposite side of the large room I felt compelled to extend my hand towards him as I prayed; "Lord, meet him. Praise You and thank You for what You are doing in him." I felt a liberty and joy in praying that I rarely experienced. Suddenly, something unexplainable happened. As I stretched out my hand towards Mr. Sarthe and prayed, God took hold of my hand! Yes, that is exactly what it felt like. A huge warm surge of tingling power flooded my out-stretched hand and then rushed up my arm. I put my hands together and the warmth spread into my left hand and spread up the arm till my whole body was bathed in glorious, tingling, powerful warmth. At the same time my spirit was filled with awe, God had come! I hardly dared speak or breathe. Foolishly I said to myself, *"I wonder if this is the Holy Spirit?"* The thought was soon swamped by a welling up of love and worship that so engulfed me that I was no longer aware of the room or everyone present, it was only me face to face with my God. The precious Lord filled my whole vision.

The meeting was drawing to a close. A hymn was announced and David McKee's fine tenor voice led the singing as everyone stood; except me. I was lost in the Lord and so elated in my spirit that I thought I could never stand up. I just wanted to stay locked into His presence. The Holy Spirit then spoke to me so plainly that it could have been an audible voice. I was arrested as He said, "The Holy Spirit is given to those who obey Me." I thought He was saying this because I must stand up, so I said, "Yes Lord, I will stand up." I stood up completely enraptured with the Lord. Although I held the hymn book I didn't sing the words as the worship of my heart was so full. The Lord opened up the heavenly realm and overwhelmed me so that I felt disconnected from my surroundings. I swayed a little and feared I would fall over, so with a deliberate effort I collected myself, straightened up, wrenching my thoughts back to the room.

As I stiffened myself and grabbed the chair in front of me, it was as if the Lord turned His face from me. No longer was I basking in the warmth of His presence, in that moment a cold desolation settled upon me. He had gone! We have all experienced those occasions when the warm summer sun is obliterated from view for a moment by a drifting cloud. Suddenly there is a chill in the air as shade takes the place of brilliant sunshine. That's how it felt. He was gone. Immediately I rose up in my spirit and ran after Him. My feet didn't move from where I was standing, but everything within me pursued Him with desperate urgency. From the depths of my being I cried out as in my spirit—I lunged out chasing after Him—"Lord, Lord don't leave me, I yield everything." Then from those same deep places of my spirit I heard myself shout out at the top of my voice, "Jesus"! The cry rang round the room but first it resounded in heavenly places. The Lord heard and He came. The Holy Spirit deluged me, coming upon me with such force that every cell of my body was impacted. I fell flat on my face on the floor. The singing wavered for a moment, but the company continued stoically to the end, trying not to notice that anything had happened! As I lay there, the Holy Spirit flooded upon me; wave after wave after wave of the love of God passed through my body. The burning, tingling sensation felt like low voltage electric shocks.

My spirit was utterly absorbed with the person of Jesus. He was altogether lovely. I was consumed with love for Him and could only say "Jesus! Jesus!" Lying on the floor the sheer awe and wonder of His beauty astonished me. He appeared to be standing just before my prostrate body. I reached out my hands and it was as if I was touching His feet. He was so tangible and real. I thought of Mary holding the Master's feet. "Oh My Jesus how I love You! You have come; You have not left me desolate. You have manifested Yourself to me!" I did not see Him with my physical eyes but the manner in which I saw Him was just as real.

The meeting closed and the room emptied, with everyone walking round my body lying in the doorway. I was quite oblivious to all the activity. Great surges of Holy Spirit power charged through my body again and again. Only Jesus filled my vision. Time had no meaning. It could have been for an eternity that I lay enraptured, prostrate before Him. Heavenly realities were so tangible. I felt I was floating, lifted out of my body holding the feet of Jesus. The reality of His presence was so real. He was standing by my head. Again and again I was amazed that it was possible to know Jesus in such a way this side of heaven. "Jesus! Jesus!" Surely this is heaven, I thought.

When I reluctantly sat up a small group were sitting about me, almost as if they were warming their hands around a fire! Biswanath, our converted Brahmin friend, gazed at me. Lolling back in his chair that supported his paralyzed body, he exclaimed to Alan, "Now I believe in the baptism of the Holy Spirit. Her face glows like the face of an angel." Many years later Alan told me that he had felt a little fearful that night when he was near me. He said there was such a holy presence of Jesus.

David McKee was propping himself on the edge of the table. He was obviously tired. Still feeling disconnected from earthly things, I 'floated' over to David and said, "I've not spoken in tongues." The remark seemed quite irrelevant. Without waiting for his reply my eyes met Alan's. He was looking at me strangely. I felt such a love towards him and longed to catch him up into all I was experiencing. When I had fallen to the floor, Alan's immediate thought had been to pick me up, but the Spirit checked him. Although it was shocking to see his wife lying on the floor in a public meeting, he knew it was God at work. This was before the days when people are often 'slain in the Spirit' in meetings.

No one wanted to leave. It was very late. The familiar noise of traffic and the honking of horns was quieting. The pavements were already lined with sleeping bodies. I felt as if I was walking on air as I drifted down the spiral stairs with Alan to his motorbike. We made for home completely unaware of the glorious joys that awaited us before we saw the dawn.

CHAPTER 21

LOVING DELIVERANCE

For months Alan had been desperately seeking God for himself. The Week to Seek God was as much an appointment with the promises of God for him, as it proved to be for me. Alan's journey to that point was somewhat different to mine as the Lord graciously led him into freedom. Alan and John had enjoyed each other's fellowship for over a year in their common quest to be baptized in the Holy Spirit. Days were spent together in retreat in Matheran, a pleasant hill resort near Bombay in an attempt to settle the issue once and for all. They had hoped 'something' would suddenly happen which would banish all their doubts and fears and give them the ability to lead the people with confidence.

One evening Alan walked through a draped doorway in the retreat bungalow when his head touched the curtain rod and brought the curtains tumbling down upon him. He was in such a state of expectancy that as he sat on the floor enveloped in the curtains he thought, *"Oh! It has happened!"* Then sat there laughing till his sides ached.

"If only God would send the Spirit in one mighty 'whoosh' from heaven", Alan thought. Though the mighty 'whoosh' did not come, Alan was not disappointed when he returned home. The Lord had spoken and brought him to a new settled place of faith. He believed that the baptism of the Holy Spirit was potentially his and now he was prepared to wait in faith for the manifestation.

When the meetings began with David McKee, no one was more committed or more expectant than Alan, so he was keenly disappointed when pressing demands at Gospel Literature Service prevented him from being in the first two morning prayer meetings. On Wednesday he determined to get to the prayer meeting even if he were late. Panting after hurrying up the steep stairs, he crept into the long room and eased himself into the nearest vacant chair. Cross legged, sitting on the floor beside him was a little sari-clad Indian woman praying in tongues. She was quite oblivious of anyone in the room or that she was infuriating Alan by her continual mumbling. However much he endeavored to ignore her, he found he could not. He had so looked forward to the prayer meeting, expecting it to be the same glorious but orderly time as usual, not this. To him, it was quite improper and out of order. More than one person was praying at a time and the noise level was certainly higher than was comfortable. Then David McKee said, "God does not want to see the back of your neck, lift up your faces!" Alan buried his face more deeply in his hands and feeling increasingly uncomfortable, wondered how he could get out. Eyeing the door he decided that to leave would draw more attention to him than he wanted. He had to stay put.

Eventually the proceedings drew to a close. David McKee stood up and opened his Bible. He read from the second book of Samuel, chapter six; the story of King David bringing home the ark of God to Zion. The word says, Michal his wife looked from her window as the procession passed by and she saw King David worshipping and dancing before the Lord with all his might. She despised and mocked him for his liberty. David's reply was that his liberty was before the Lord not before the people and he had no intention of changing! David McKee then read verse twenty-three slowly and deliberately, "Michal the daughter of Saul had no children and was barren to the day of her death." Then he added, "Because she was more concerned about the people than with God, Michal was barren all her life." This remark went like an arrow through Alan's defenses of traditionalism and formality. He suddenly saw before him the specter of a barren Christian life.

A hush fell upon the meeting, then David turned to Alan and said, "Brother, will you close in prayer?"

Turmoil raged in Alan's mind as everyone sat passively in the penetrating silence waiting for him to pray. He knew it was God who had cornered him. The choice was plain—either he could be like fruitful David, or like barren Michal. "Lord, he cried in his heart, I can't bear to be barren, help me." As he wept, out tumbled his honest confession.

"Oh God! You have found me out. I have despised those here who worshipped God in their liberty and I have refused to bend. Lord, I have behaved like Michal. Forgive me; I don't want to be barren for the rest of my life. I will do whatever You say, but make me like David."

Alan's painfully honest prayer struck a familiar chord in other hearts that morning. The awesome fear of the Lord came down and gripped others who also had a critical spirit.

The next morning Alan went to the prayer meeting with a determination that he would submit to whatever the Lord said. Although the liberty in the meeting was greater than the day before nothing seemed as objectionable, till the Lord said, "Raise your hands and worship Me." Alan stiffened. Why was this so difficult? He could not explain it to himself. He knew the raising of the hands in worship was in the Bible, he could find no reason for his objection, but regardless he felt very uncomfortable. Alan had come to the meeting determined to submit to the Spirit so slowly he raised his hand to shoulder level and then tentatively pushed it a little higher, at which time he was sure that everybody in the room must be watching him. Though acutely embarrassed, he made up his mind to obey the Lord. A little higher and it was straight up above his head. Now the problem was he didn't know how to bring it down! Alan said, "It felt like a huge tree above the forest." At that point the Lord snapped an indefinable bondage and he was free.

In the following months Alan repeatedly had to re-exert his liberty to be free in worship. The bondage would close in upon him trying to prevent his liberty in worship by raising his hands to the Lord. For many, that will sound strange, but the bondage was real. The freedom Alan gained had far greater implications than raising his hands in worship. It was barely noticeable at first, but with Alan's increased liberty to worship the Lord, he experienced a progressive freedom pervading his whole character.

Strangely, after months of seeking for the baptism in the Holy Spirit and enjoying times when faith was high, there was still a nagging doubt in Alan's mind concerning its reality. He continued to toss theological objections around in his head and would ask himself questions. Was he filled with the Spirit when he was converted or is there some other infilling necessary? Are tongues really part of the infilling and how will I know if I am baptized in the Holy Spirit?

During the Week to Seek God, following another such session of questioning and doubting, Alan began reading Smith Wigglesworth's book "*Ever Increasing Faith*". His eyes focused upon one sentence, "If you have any doubts, the best way to deal with doubts is to take the Word of God and shout it with all your might. That will free you and drive the devil right off your back! Take your doubts and have a good shout!"

That morning Alan planned to go to the morning meeting held in the Brethren Assembly, the home of orthodox, fundamental evangelicalism in Bombay. David McKee who was an Irish Presbyterian missionary would not normally have received an invitation to this Assembly, but because of his reputation as an excellent Bible teacher of great scholarship, it had been extended to him and the Assembly hosted a morning meeting during the Week to Seek God.

The Lord challenged Alan. "I want you to go to the meeting this morning and settle your doubts once and for all. Go and shout, I believe in the baptism of the Holy Spirit and I am seeking God to meet me this way." When Alan told the story later he said, "I told the Lord, Oh Lord I couldn't do that, I'd die. And the Lord replied to him, "Exactly! That is what I'm after. I want you to die and I will set you free." Alan went to the meeting as a man going to his own execution. Since the episode with Michal and her despising of David's freedom, Alan had a greater fear to disobey God than his fear of the people. Deep down in his heart he knew these directives were the firm hand of a loving Father determined to set him free.

Alan had no idea how he would be able to shout his declaration. On previous mornings the meetings had been very structured with no interaction. When he arrived he looked about the congregation apprehensively. Every 'sound brother' whom he would have preferred not to be there was present including many of the Assembly members and they wouldn't appreciate what Alan was going to shout!

The moment came. David McKee was about to preach. He hesitated for a moment and said, "I think this morning we will have a time of testimony. If anyone has anything to say, now is your opportunity."

Alan knew that was his cue. He stood up and said, "The Lord has told me to shout something."

Quite unperturbed David said, "Go ahead Brother. Shout if that is what the Lord has said."

Alan opened his mouth and let out a 'shout' but it came out squeaky because he was so nervous. "I believe in the baptism of the Holy Spirit and I am waiting for God to bless me in this way!"

He sat down to an embarrassing silence. Recounting the story Alan says, "It was terrible!" The respectable evangelical Alan Vincent had died never to rise again. Alan's chains were broken, he was free.

Sometime later, Alan realized none of these painful dealings of the Lord were without their cause. When praying he had always been careful to pray in such a way as would appear sound and acceptable to those present. His preaching was inhibited by the desire to please and say what was expedient. His fear of man and his desire to please men were dealt with in one violent stroke. Alan was free. He left the meeting a new man.

The Lord was answering his prayers. He had longed for a deep work of the Spirit in his life so the Lord in His mercy continued to put pressure upon the areas in Alan's life that demanded change. More cleansing would come and more bondage would be broken before the Spirit was to fall upon him.

At the final Friday evening meeting, the glorious occasion when the Spirit fell upon me, Alan had been riveted by the prophetic word, "Rend your hearts and not your garments." A fearful awe fell upon him, his heart opened up to the Spirit as so many were pouring out their deep confessions of sin. It was not a time for covering sin, the search light of the Spirit was examining every deep place within hearts. Publically he poured out his confessions so that he left the meeting that night with a light heart, thrilled by the presence of the Holy Spirit.

Alan cut the engine of his motorbike as it turned into the alleyway, leading to our flat. Bumping over water pipes and broken drains it glided to a standstill. I had no recollection of the half hour's journey home; the time had been spent in the Lord's presence on the back of the bike.

The windows of our bedroom were wide open to catch any breath of a breeze on that still hot night. We undressed in the dark then lay down on our old ex-army, iron framed beds. The ancient wire mesh was held together with ropes. The imbedded knots made familiar lumps and bumps in the thin mattress. Sleep was far from our thoughts.

As we lay upon our beds we prayed. The atmosphere was alive with the power of God. I kept my eyes closed. I did not want to see natural things. My eyes were looking into the Spirit realm to see the true realities. I still felt as if I was floating; somehow I was not connected with my body. This strange feeling lasted for about five days, though during that time I was caring for my home and family.

As we laid there, Alan prayed "Lord, I am so thankful for the way in which You have met Eileen, You know we have always done everything together, please send Your Spirit upon me." The presence of Holy Spirit began to fill the room; every sense was alerted as Alan became acutely aware as He drew close. Soon Alan was shut into an intimate visitation of God and quite oblivious to my presence. Intensely aware of God's awful holiness Alan lay still, barely breathing. In spite of all his longings to be baptized in the Holy Spirit, now as God drew near, he stiffened and closed up inside. The Holy Spirit withdrew and, to him, the bedroom seemed empty and ordinary again.

Oh, how desolate Alan felt. He cried, "Lord, I didn't mean to drive You away; I cannot understand myself, forgive me. Please come!" Time passed. Whether it was five minutes or an hour Alan did not know, then just as quietly as the Holy Spirit had departed, now graciously He returned. Gently, like dew from heaven, the room again filled with the pure, consuming presence of God. To move, speak, or even to breathe seemed almost irreverent.

Alan was resolute this time. He lay on his bed basking in the presence of the Lord and determined he would not be fearful. As the Spirit began to fall upon him he aggressively went out to possess the Lord. Not that he moved from his bed, but in his heart he presumptuously snatched. Bewildered and desolate, again Alan was left bereft as the Holy Spirit withdrew. Patiently the Lord showed Alan that he cannot possess the Spirit, but the Spirit must possess him.

Each encounter taught valuable lessons and brought fresh revelation of the character of the Holy Spirit. Alan prayed, "Lord, I will neither run from You nor grab presumptuously. Teach me how to yield and receive."

A third time the Spirit filled the room. As He came near, Alan submitted joyously, receiving all that God wanted to pour upon him. Then wave after wave of the power of the Holy Spirit flowed through his body, he said it felt like low level electricity. Even his bed trembled as power fell upon him. Flooded with love and filled to overflowing with the precious Holy Spirit, Alan knew himself to be personally loved and cherished by God. Such intimate love has never ceased to amaze him so that he continually rejoices in the wonder of this relationship.

Throughout these amazing visitations Alan was locked into the presence of God in such a personal way that he remained unaware of me next to him. I was still caught up in the Holy Spirit myself praying and rejoicing and so thankful for all the Lord was doing. Then something changed. Alan began to speak out in prophecy by the Spirit that was resting upon him. Though Alan was speaking we both knew we were listening to the word of God being personally delivered to both of us. The words were specific detailing the calling upon our lives. He was saying things that we hardly understood. "I have called you into an apostolic ministry."

As we dozed in the early hours of the morning, there were signs that others were waking. Like most huge cities it is said of Bombay that it never sleeps, but it does have waking noises. The packs of roaming dogs have their last skirmish making blood curdling noises in heated battles, before they flop down to sleep. Incredibly loud throat-clearing noises echo round the buildings, all part of the early morning ablutions. Then the vegetable *walla* gets down from his 'bed' that now reverts to its day use, a cart headed to the wholesale market to get supplies for the early morning sales. The sounds of waking Bombay drifted through our open windows; it sounded like every other day, but today was entirely new, we were never to be the same again.

CHAPTER 22

LIVING IN THE HOLY SPIRIT

We had been seeking God for almost two years and we both had huge expectations of what this new life should bring. The theme of revival had fuelled our prayer meetings and driven us in our search. We devoured books on past revivals and outpourings of the Holy Spirit in many nations. Each reading raised our expectation for such glorious things to happen among us. We had not sought the Holy Spirit just for a personal experience; our longings were for a mighty visitation upon our city. We longed for revival and everything the word conjured up in our minds, with mighty ingatherings of souls and glorious miraculous power loosed upon whole societies.

It is good to dream, strategize, work and pray for God-sized ambitions but then we have to face the harsh reality of our everyday lives. The first step to change our world begins right here, living His life by the power of the Holy Spirit in whatever circumstances we find ourselves.

Alan spent most days in the Gospel Literature Service press. There in his ordinary daily demands he felt the impact of what the Lord had done for him; he knew he was a new man. Nothing in his outward circumstances had changed, he still interacted with the same people every day, but now Alan found a new super-abundant supply of love, a love that would accommodate people with their idiosyncrasies that just days before, had been painful to endure. The strain went out of relationships and joy came in. This was not an earth moving revival but it was a flow of God-life into daily circumstances.

This *agape* love wasn't just confined to life in the Press; it was flowing all the time. Alan surprised himself when he went to buy bananas from the old woman who sat with her basket at the corner of the street; looking at her he felt overflowing, loving compassion for the toothless old grandmother! The whole world became a transformed place as he looked at it through different eyes; eyes of interest, love and concern.

My hunger for the Holy Spirit had been fuelled by an insatiable desire to experience the love of God pouring through my life. I was desperate for this; I wanted to be able to love the unlovely, but more than that, I wanted to be a loving person and not cause offense or pain to others. I came to understand that *agape* love would continue to love, even when there was no response. I was constantly aware of my own deep need for such a love. Too often I had said of myself, "I'm not good at loving, I don't know how to give love or receive it." My continual cry had been, "Let me experience Romans 5:5, the love of God poured out into my heart by the Holy Spirit."

Early the following day the Lord allowed me the joy of His amazing answer to my prayer. I was walking in a narrow passageway behind someone whom I had always found difficult to love. Normally I would be 'working overtime' trying to keep the relationship upon an even keel, but that day, I was swept through with such an abundance of love, Romans 5:5 happened! The love of God was poured out into my heart by the Holy Spirit! I was amazed at the depth and emotion of love that poured out of me into this wonderful person. My heart was melted. I knew it was God.

Love gripped both of us in new ways for the city of Bombay. Our hearts were broken for the lost trusting in their idols and false gods, seeking fortune tellers and workers of magic, bound by demons and gripped by generational iniquity and sin. Love charged our prayers and made us yet more determined to speak to all who would listen.

Nobody had told us that once the Holy Spirit fell upon us that we would have a new Bible! Now, as we read well known passages they came alive with fresh understanding and in an intimate way we experienced the Holy Spirit leading us into all truth. We welcomed the heightened ability to hear the Spirit and receive revelation.

About two weeks after our baptism in the Holy Spirit Alan said, "I am speaking in tongues, well let's say I'm making noises, but I'm not sure it's the real thing." That night he crept from the bedroom and went to meet with the Lord. Worshipping he spoke in tongues; but again doubted that it was the true gift. With no fear of interruption he set up the tape recorder and spoke the strange sounds into the microphone. After running the tape back he listened with an analytical ear. Thinking aloud he said, "Yes it sounds like a language, it has syntax; but is it tongues? I still don't know."

Within a few days I was also speaking in tongues. One morning when reading and praying, I felt sure that the gift of tongues was mine and all I needed to do was to launch out and speak. Opening my mouth I began to say various sounds. Carefully I listened to myself. It was fascinating. Nothing spectacular was happening, the heavens didn't open and the Spirit didn't fall. Again and again I spoke but it was the same few words. I began to recognize them and thought all I was doing was repeating the same sounds or was I just mimicking the various languages which were about me everyday? With a deliberate effort I tried to shake off the suggestion, but it had left its mark. My time of quiet abruptly ended. Duncan's tricycle rammed into the bedroom door and simultaneously the flat reverberated with the yell of the vegetable *walla* outside the kitchen door.

Throughout the day I repeated the same sounds without any strong conviction that I was speaking in tongues. Simple faith told me, *"You have what you asked for; tongues."* But reason said, *"Can this foolishness be a gift of the Holy Spirit?"* Both Alan and I continued in this double minded state for a few days. We didn't know anyone who spoke in tongues so we could only turn to the Lord for an answer. We decided to ask Him to prove the genuineness of the gift by giving each of us an interpretation; first to me as Alan spoke and then to Alan as I spoke my few words. It was strange how embarrassed we felt to speak in tongues in front of one another. It is all right to make foolish noises by oneself, but we discovered there was a death in displaying our foolishness!

The iron frame dug in our stomachs as we knelt by the bed. Alan prayed in his tongue. The Spirit of God came down and engulfed us in His glorious presence. The whole room seemed full of God. Waiting, we expected some interpretation but nothing came. The silence continued into awkwardness; then it was my turn. Self-consciously I spoke. Breathless in the intense presence of God we waited for Alan to be given the interpretation. Again, nothing happened, but strange to say there was no disappointment for the Lord had imperceptibly given His peace concerning His gift. His own presence had assured us that the sounds we spoke were the authentic gift of God.

That encounter became a landmark occasion in our lives and never again did we entertain doubts concerning the good gifts of the Holy Spirit. The putting away of doubts and unbelief had an immediate effect upon the gift. Instead of a few stammering words, a language began to flow and my testimony became "He who speaks in tongues edifies himself."

The same evening an enthusiastic group gathered for the prayer meeting in our tiny flat. Furniture was removed to make space for all who squeezed through the door. Joyously we praised the Lord; it didn't matter that we were making a lot of noise, it was normal to make a lot of noise in our building! A strong sense of the Spirit was upon me, my heart beat faster and I felt a kind of pressure while my spirit was taken up with the joy of Jesus. I opened my mouth and in a loud clear voice spoke out in my new tongue. Such a thing had never happened in our meetings before. In hushed awe we waited for the interpretation. Inside I was praising and glorifying God. The silence became too long, so I assumed that I should give the interpretation, because the word says in 1 Cor.14:13, "*anyone who speaks in a tongue should pray that he may interpret what he says.*" I spilled out all the praise that was in my heart. The 'amens' and 'hallelujahs' covered my uncomfortable feeling that I had been too hasty and that the interpretation was yet to come. A few songs later Alan spoke out a most beautiful message. I knew without doubt that this was the interpretation.

The meeting thinned out and people reluctantly made for home. John, Reta and one or two others held back. Everything about John, even his huge lumberjack frame, spoke gentleness and humility. It was he who spoke first. "What did you think about the interpretation this evening? If you don't mind me saying I think the word that Alan gave had the Spirit's confirmation resting upon it. I feel that was the real interpretation." There was an immediate general agreement.

Then Alan sheepishly confessed, "As soon as Eileen gave the tongue, a few thoughts were strongly impressed upon my mind, but I couldn't quite pluck up courage to speak them out."

I added, "The silence seemed so long that I thought, 'if no one is going to give the interpretation, perhaps I must,' and that was the result. But I do admit I had an uncomfortable suspicion that I had been too hasty." We were all learning! Patiently the Lord dealt with us leading us out into ministry and teaching us even through our mistakes.

Since the outpouring of the Holy Spirit John and Reta Hutchinson continued to lead the church. Then the time came for them to return to Canada with their growing family making it necessary to find a new pastor for the church. Alan was unable to accept the invitation because we planned to return to England five months later ourselves. In the meantime he agreed to fill the position while attempts were made to find a permanent pastor. Alan added the full preaching burden of the church to his already demanding schedule, but the Lord blest him in the ministry. The numbers in the church continued to grow and there was a real sense of God's approval resting upon all we did. The gifts of the Spirit became accepted in the mid-week prayer meeting and the sick were always prayed for. At each Sunday service the unconverted were being drawn in and hardly a week went by without conversions.

Baptizing the converts became quite a problem, as there always was a chronic water shortage. After the baptisms we didn't dare empty the pool as it took a full week to re-fill from the slow dribble that came only a few hours each day. To keep the water reasonably wholesome we just added a little more chlorine.

The excitement and joy of walking with the Lord in those days resists comparison. "You shall receive power when the Holy Spirit has come upon you," became evident in many lives. We were those who believed and expected to see 'signs following'. A Hindu man was healed of tuberculosis after he had been discharged as a hopeless case from the local hospital. A woman in the Naval hospital was saved from certain death when Christ appeared and touched her. A continuous hemorrhage following child birth immediately stopped. She was discharged from the hospital and gave testimony in the church. The demon-possessed were all about us but never before were we so blatantly confronted with the problem till one Sunday evening. The Lord intended to stretch our faith and bring us into a new place of authority over demons.

Alan had just stood up to preach, when a street boy about fifteen years old wandered into the service. His eyes were glazed and he didn't seem to know where he was. Everybody's attention was fixed upon him as he ambled to the front of the church. From the pulpit Alan commanded the boy in the name of Jesus to sit down and to be quiet. He obeyed. Afterwards we discovered that the boy didn't understand any English but the spirits within him understood the power of the name of Jesus. I wish I could tell you that the boy was gloriously delivered, but unfortunately, it was not so. Every time we prayed with him he went into a deep sleep. Hours later he would wake with the same haunted animal expression in his eyes. After a few days his brother took him away. Many years later we encountered the same sleep inducing spirit in someone else but then, we saw deliverance.

The second and third attempts at deliverance were no more successful, but God was using the situation to train us and establish His authority in us. We were passing through a wilderness experience of testing and temptation. We were face to face with the devil and he was intent on stopping our advance against his kingdom of darkness. He tried to put doubts in our hearts concerning the power of the name of Jesus and the anointing that we had received. We battled against his lies with the sword of the Spirit, the Word of God. This was a new kind of attack, but what power was let loose as we followed the example of Jesus and fought the good fight of faith. Doubts fled giving place to the knowledge of the certain victory that is ours in the mighty Name of Jesus. We saw that all the disappointments and failure had been allowed by God to bring us to a place of faith where we would have a good reputation with the devil! We never wanted the devil to be able to say of us, "And who are you?" We came out of our wilderness experience to see the triumph of the Name of Jesus over the powers of hell demonstrated again and again.

CHAPTER 23

TRAVELS FAR AND WIDE

Alan had always been a scholar, always ready to study whatever the subject required. So when he became a Christian it was natural for him to become a student of the Word. He would spend hours in preparation and because of his powerful expositions in the Word he became a sought after speaker especially for student meetings in those early days. He considered pursuing a degree in Biblical Studies at London University when we returned to England. Frequently he had felt belittled when questioned, "Which Bible College did you go to?" so he thought to remedy this situation and make himself more acceptable in church circles.

During the months that we had been seeking God for the power of the Holy Spirit an invitation arrived for Alan to go to Calcutta to The Carey Baptist Church, named after the pioneer missionary William Carey. Alan was invited to minister at a Camp for students from the tribal regions in Assam and Nagaland. He was excited at the prospect of teaching the hungry group of young people. Sitting that afternoon in what had been William Carey's bedroom trying to get his message for the evening, Alan had a conversation with the Lord and told him of his desire for Bible training. Lovingly, the Lord came to Alan. His presence was so real that it was as if He sat on the bed next to him. The Lord made it clear that Bible college was not in His plan for Alan. Then in a magnificent way He proceeded to open the Word with such revelation that not only fed Alan, but enabled him to teach. As the Lord withdrew He said, "I have sent you to feed My sheep not My giraffes!" Alan has never forgotten that; he knows he could become too cerebral given the right environment.

Bombay in 1966 had a large student population and many from the tribal areas in north India made the Baptist church their home. Vamouso

Phizo, a leader among them, invited us to minister at the annual gathering of the Chakhestan Baptist Association in the heart of the Naga Hills, which bordered Burma in the far northeast of India. This tribal area was Vamouso's home but it was caught in the middle of warfare between the Indian army and the rebel army of the freedom movement. At the same time, the most magnificent outpouring of God's Spirit was taking place. Thousands were coming to Christ and the virgin soil was proving to be the most fruitful. We were excited at the thought of going there, but again we had a problem of how to pay for such an expensive journey. We did not have money for the train fares for ourselves and the children; Rachel was now six years old and Duncan three.

We prayed again and again and every time we came to the same conclusion; we should go. Plans were made; with the little money we had, we bought one-way tickets for ourselves and the two children. We would trust God to provide for the return! The day came to begin the three day journey and we were at peace. Vamouso was to meet us with entry permits at the final leg of the journey after a flight from Calcutta, but unknown to us the permit had to be presented in Calcutta, so were not allowed to board the flight. We sat near the plane steps waiting while people asked questions and tried to help us. We prayed.

An hour went by and all this time the plane was delayed. Although we had explained our situation to dozens of people nothing was happening. Then suddenly there was a lot of activity. Hurriedly, a red carpet was put down and a group of security personnel appeared, but nobody took any notice of us. An official said, "The plane is being delayed, waiting for the Chief Minister of Assam." Finally he arrived and noticed us waiting. To our surprise he asked, "What is your trouble?" Hearing our situation he took a sheet of paper and signed a personal permission for us to land in Gauhati! We were quickly ushered down the red carpet onto the plane and as soon as the Chief Minister was seated we took off.

We knew we had had a miracle; God intended us to go to Nagaland. We expected Vamouso to meet us from the plane with the entry document for Nagaland and then to escort us on the last leg of the journey. For some reason he didn't come and we were very conspicuous in this high security area. Soon the police were questioning us and would not allow us to complete the journey without the special visa for Nagaland. It would have been simple if there were telephones but such refinements were not to be had. I guess we understood before we left home that this journey would be another occasion to stretch our faith!

Eventually we were escorted by the police to the home of an ex-government minister of the Lushai people. We were virtually under house arrest until we could produce the right papers! Our hosts gave us tribal hospitality. They were very gracious. The house was in the process of being built and there was barely any furniture. When we asked about the toilet, with a wave of the hand we were directed to 'out there' but despite the language difficulties they were wonderful to us. After a week of praying and waiting, the papers were obtained from Delhi and we were on our way up the mountain. The Lord arranged special transport for us; we were driven in the Nagaland Government Medical Minister's jeep and spent our first night in his official residence in Kohima! Duncan at three years old was thrilled with the soldiers walking up and down outside. He thought it was like Buckingham Palace in London.

The next day we set out again. We had come to a very primitive area and were astonished to see a man wearing just a loin cloth and carrying a spear come out of the jungle ahead of us. He could have walked out of the stone-age. Every moment there was something new to see, smell or cause you to say, "Wow!" The scenery was remarkable. There were bamboo forests with birds I had never seen before; swift flowing rivers and precarious bamboo "bridges" swaying in the wind. The exotic flowers and butterflies were a delight; I was having a feast! There was so much to see but too little time to take it all in as we whisked by in the vehicle.

Fortunately the children enjoyed the ride, but were beginning to get hungry and there were no restaurants. As we passed through a village, people waved and a lady came running and pressed a bag of cooked beans into our hands. Beans made a good Naga snack. We were soon to sample Naga curries and mountains of rice. Now we were used to Indian food but by all standards, this Naga curry was hot. The mountains of rice helped us get it down.

As we approached the host village, our driver pointed out a row of white painted posts like little heads on sticks arranged at the entrance of the village. He went on to explain that historically the Nagas were head hunters. The heathen customs of village life required that a young man, to qualify as a warrior, had to raid another village and bring back a head! Each white post represented a head that had been brought back in triumph by one of these warriors. Next to the heads was a huge hollowed out tree trunk that used to store the local brew. The warriors would gather and drink this concoction till they were drunk; it was part of life and preparation for raiding another village.

In the evening, after a day of fascinating travel through mountains and along torturous roads with army check posts and guns trained upon us, we arrived at the convention in the dark. Every moment we learned something surprising. The meetings were being held in the open air and there was no lighting or seating. We were encouraged to grab a pile of straw to sit upon as the ground was cold and damp. As our eyes became accustomed to the dark we could make out a huge gathering of people all sitting on the ground huddled up in shawls. Once the sun went down the temperature dropped to near freezing. Soon we were introduced to the heating system, a small portable charcoal burner that the locals put under their shawls making them like a heated tent.

On the platform, the leaders were exhorting the people and then someone said, "Let's pray!" Suddenly a roar went up from those dark hillsides as all at once those we could barely see opened their mouths and poured out heartfelt cries to God. This was so far from the Baptist church prayer meetings we had been used to; I couldn't help thinking these people prayed more in 10 minutes than the church at home had ever prayed in its life! We were among a people experiencing the beginnings of revival and who were not steeped in western church ways. Their example stayed with me throughout our days in India.

We moved our belongings into the tiny school room that was to be our accommodation for the next few days. It had a dirt floor and wooden shutters covered the opening that served as a window. The 'bed' that took up most of the space was a small school blackboard placed upon four posts. As you can imagine we wondered how this would work as a bed for all of us. Nagas are small people but our family could not be described so. I gathered armfuls of straw to give the 'bed' a little padding and we found innovative ways of sleeping in our confined quarters.

Alan preached many times to the wonderful believers; a highlight was preaching at a festival in a village where the majority was not Christian. We were given the most amazing display of traditional dance. The dancers were dressed in very colorful shawls wrapped about them like skirts and their bodies were decorated with beads and shells. The warrior dance was riveting as the young men sung and shouted war cries finishing in a yell as they symbolically went off to battle. As Alan gave the invitation to be saved the son of the village headman came and gave his life to Christ. He was going to be a warrior for Jesus!

Our time in Nagaland was drawing to a close. We had had very little time to think about how we were to get back to Bombay; we still did not have any means to buy train tickets, we had not seen money since we had been in Nagaland! Pastor Dupor Vasa, the leader of the churches took us to his home for the night on our way back to the railway station. Graciously he gave us a bed for the night and we were ready to sleep but he wanted to talk. He told us that God had spoken to him and we watched as he carefully pulled up a floor board, reached in and brought out a box. Opening it up, he took out a fist full of rupees and handed them to Alan. We were astonished and could hardly speak. Here was the miracle we had been waiting for, Jehovah Jireh knew exactly what we needed and without us saying a word He spoke to His servant. As we counted the money there was enough for the journey and some to spare. Before we laid our heads down to sleep we were praising God for His amazing faithfulness. He had told us to go to Nagaland and allowed us to be tested so that we would see Him do miracles. Again the Lord reminded me, "You will never know the God of the impossible until you are in an impossible situation."

Now that the power of the Spirit had fallen upon us, it seemed that the Lord sent out a 'memo' saying, "Invite Alan and Eileen Vincent!" Invitations began to come from mission stations in many places where the missionaries wanted to be filled with the Holy Spirit, even if that terminology and experience went against their mission policy or church doctrine. A supernatural hunger had been stirred in the hearts of these hardworking, dedicated and selfless people, most of them women.

We travelled to many towns and mission stations in Maharashtra, the state where we lived and far beyond, even into Nepal and Bangladesh in response to some calls. We visited ministries that had struggled for decades, but who had come to the realization that their only hope was the power of God. Deep problems in the churches and relationship difficulties on many mission stations now became intolerable and had to be resolved. It was God's time. The Lord granted us days of miracles; many sicknesses were healed and Alan preached the word with power and great application. It was during this time that my prophetic preaching and teaching ministry developed with authority over evil spirits and the anointing to bring people into the fullness of the Spirit. All the women missionaries in one mission were filled with the Spirit, the hunger was so great. Unfortunately most of the men continued their doubting and questioning.

Little did we know that God was preparing the small, divided church of India to stand alone and to take responsibility for its own affairs. For many years the major denominations had been involved in a church unification movement. Their deliberations were finalized in 1970 after years of discussion. This birthed the Church of North India and the Church of South India. This was God's divine timing because the government established new visa regulations so that the congregations could no longer depend upon the foreign missionaries.

Looking back, it is evident that the unification movement was part of the preparation of the church for the days ahead; but equally, so was the revitalizing of the spiritual life of missionaries who in turn brought renewal to their spheres of the church. No one knew that very soon many of them would be forced to leave India and others would not be able to return. The outpouring of the Holy Spirit in many diverse places laid a foundation of Spirit-filled indigenous leaders, who in the coming years were crucial to the evangelization of India.

CHAPTER 24

COUNTING PENNIES IN THE MIDDLE OF PLENTY

We came to the end of our fruitful and demanding days in the Baptist church and made our emotional goodbyes. It was time to go back to England. We had been in India for three and a half years and it changed us forever. Most of us rarely share the deepest longings and dreams that the Lord has put in our hearts. Sometimes it is only as they begin to blossom that we even grasp—I was born for this! Mission life was for me. These first years in India were a preparation, yes, but more than that, they let me taste future possibilities and ruined me for the ordinary. The Spirit lit a passion in me for revival. I loved to see the Spirit fall and do whatever He wanted. The time in India had given me opportunity to minister in many unstructured meetings where the Spirit moved freely. I wondered what England would hold for me now.

It was August 1966 when we joined the Galileo Galilei, a huge ship, which was to take us back to Europe. After examining our cabins we went up onto the deck watching as the ropes were cast off and we drew out of port. So many memories flooded our minds and so many faces came before us in those few wrenching moments. The neat docks gave an unusual view of Bombay; the familiar sights, smells and streets seemed a million miles away. We were leaving a life that had woven itself deep into our hearts; it had become a place where we belonged. In those last poignant moments, as the dock faded from view the Lord said clearly into my heart, "You will return in three years."

Life was challenging as we reestablished our lives in England. Sunday came and we returned to the Baptist church that we had left over three years before. We hadn't realized how much we had changed; our world perspective now made us a misfit for the local village church. For the first time we had difficulty encouraging the children to go to the Sunday school. They were accustomed to a much more vibrant style of meeting.

The following week we met with old friends. As we talked we discovered that they were hungry for the power of the Holy Spirit and wanted to see God at work in their lives. They had started a small fellowship and longed for it to be effective in evangelizing the local people. They hoped we would join them and so invited Alan to talk with the leaders. He gave them his testimony and explained he would only come if they were open to embrace the power of the Holy Spirit. A special church meeting was arranged where Alan carefully explained how they too could experience the power of Pentecost. That evening, many were baptized in the Holy Spirit. It was not immediately evident but that evening, fruitful seeds were sown that to this day have continued to influence the region.

It was one thing to have trials of faith when in India, but now home again in familiar places, surely we thought money should not be a problem. We had accepted the invitation to lead the small fellowship and they promised to help us financially when they could. It soon became obvious they could do very little. When Alan met some of his old colleagues from Kodak he learned that he could apply for a senior position in the new Royal Photographic Society that was being established in London. This appointment would certainly answer our financial needs. On one hand we felt enthusiastic when an interview was arranged but we could not completely smother a feeling of unease, *"Is this really what the Lord wants for us?"*

Alan returned elated from the interview. What an amazing opportunity was before him; all he had to do was accept the position. Yes, it would be demanding but it would be so rewarding. I felt relieved that we would not have to be wondering how we were going to manage financially. Both of us were denying the disquiet in our hearts, we didn't want to hear that voice, "This is not My way for you." After prayer Alan said he would not take the post. He was chiding himself for even going to the interview when deep inside he knew it was not for him. I was dismayed, what were we going to do? But I knew Alan was right, though I could not understand how we would manage. As Mr. Elliott would say, "I know it in my knower!" I knew the Lord would not fail us.

Week followed into week and month into month and the Lord would not permit Alan to take secular employment. In my weaker moments I chided him, "If only you would take a job our problems would be over." But I knew the Lord had another plan for us; He had a specific purpose in causing us to walk this narrow way. We were being trained to trust Him in what some would call extreme ways, because he wanted to use our faith for some mighty victories.

The home needed urgent refurbishing; the children had no winter clothes and for every daily need we were cast upon the Lord. Living from God's hand to our mouths we managed through the winter; then plans were made for Alan to return to India for ministry. Though there was no easing of our personal financial situation, Alan's expenses for his mission visit to India were immediately supplied.

When he left, the house seemed empty. I went into our study and reviewed the finances. We kept a notebook called the Lord's Account. Twenty five percent of everything we received was noted in this book and given away as the Lord directed. I looked carefully at our bank account and then noted that the sum deposited was the same amount as listed in the Lord's account. That meant that everything in our bank account belonged to the Lord. It was a sobering thought. I had no money at all and the following morning Rachel would need money for her school lunches; it was only a small sum but I had nothing!

Deliberately, I took the checkbook from the drawer and wrote one check for the whole amount as a mission gift. Carefully I placed it in an envelope, praying as I sealed it; now I was completely in the Lord's hands. He knew what I had done, He knew I had nothing. I looked at the bills, laid each of them separately on the desk, thinking, *"So that the Lord can see them."* Each one required a miracle. I backed out of the room with my eyes fixed on the bills and said to the Lord, "I am leaving those for You" and I shut the door. That evening one of the leaders from the church came with a gift that carried me through the next few days. Again I thanked God for His faithfulness and was encouraged, the Lord was watching over us.

My problems seemed more than enough, when a recent widow in the church asked if she could come to stay with me. She was desperately lonely and did not want to be alone at Easter. How could I refuse; though I hardly had a thing to set before her? The days of austerity had emptied my pantry so that I was down to the last few dry goods.

The weekend arrived. Mary came all expectant and so happy to be with us but I could not tell her of my predicament. Constantly praying that the Lord would intervene and supply our need, I thought my last hope was for a gift to come in the mail, but the postman walked past the house; there was nothing. What was I to do? The children had already emptied their money boxes; they too were asking the Lord to provide. Without money to buy meat for the traditional roast, I was at a loss; this would be a strange Easter lunch! Certainly not what Mary would expect. I carefully counted out the coins in my purse, I had enough to buy a loaf of bread and perhaps the butcher would give me scraps for the dog. Sunday lunch would have to be spaghetti with some ground meat if I could buy just a little with my remaining coins. I waited, hoping for a gift all day until it was almost time for the shops to close; then I hurried down the hill alone praying all the way.

The butcher was cleaning up the shop and the meat had already been put away in the cold room. At weekends almost every household had a roast joint of meat that the butcher individually prepared, trimming away excess meat and fat. The plentiful trimmings were sold for some well-fed dogs. Walking up to the counter I said, "Give me some dog meat please," at which the butcher carefully laid out two large sheets of paper and loaded them with multiple handfuls of off cuts from sirloin joints, legs of lamb, the trimmings from the saddle of pork and wonderful topside! Rolling it up, he handed me the heavy package, "Six pence please!" And I left for home with fresh bread and meat, of sorts.

Quietly I went into the kitchen with my huge package of dog meat and separated out the best pieces that could be for our lunch with spaghetti. The dog had enough scraps to keep her happy for days and a pile of fat was gathered into a big pot. Little did I know that the fat was going to be so useful in the following weeks. I was thanking the Lord and I prepared our meal. We had food, it was not what I would have chosen, but the

Lord was still worthy of thanks. This financial trial had been going on for a number of months and there seemed to be no end in sight. Our children, four and seven years old, did not complain but would pray with me and together we would praise the Lord when He sent us a gift. They had such simple faith.

On Sunday afternoon Mary said, "Let's all go to my house for tea; I have made a lovely Easter cake." The children were ready in no time. Big slices of cake were passed round and again I found myself praising and thanking the Lord. He was so kind to the children and it took so little to make them happy. Later that evening we returned home to find a sack of potatoes on the door step—they had been left by a local farmer. For the next weeks they were our food; potatoes in every shape and form. French fries were guaranteed to make everyone happy; now the pot of fat came into use, once rendered down we had enough to cook french fries for weeks!

After Alan arrived home from India we discovered that we had a serious infestation of wood worm in the rafters of the house and it was imperative that it be treated. This was a costly undertaking, but our difficult financial situation meant it would have to wait till the Lord changed our circumstances. It seemed totally irrational, but the Lord began to provoke us to get the wood worm treated. For about two weeks we could not get the necessity of this work out of our minds. How could we engage the contractors when we could not pay them? It seemed like madness to even contemplate doing anything about it till we had a major change in our finances. This issue became so pressing with the Lord encouraging and speaking continually till we felt compelled to take action. For days, Alan wrestled with the thought of arranging for the work to be done when we did not have the money to pay. He came to the uncomfortable conclusion that he was to engage the contractors and then the Lord would do a miracle and honor the check. We had never done such a thing before; rather we prided ourselves on being scrupulous in our handling of money.

After much heart searching the call was made; the technicians would come Friday. We agreed that Alan should hand them a check trusting the Lord to provide all that was needed by the time it was cashed. Once the job was complete and the workmen were paid, they left and the house was quiet. We had an unreasonable peace after obeying these strange instructions.

On Sunday Alan was to preach in a nearby town. Once we were in the van we all prayed that the petrol would be enough to get us to the church. Every day was a challenge. On the journey a thought kept churning over in my heart and then I blurted out, "Oh Lord I do wish I had an offering; I would love to be able to give." We clambered out of our undignified van and as we began to walk across the parking area a man came directly to me and pressed £200 into my hand! This was a huge amount of money signifying to me of how worthy He was of exceptional generous giving. I was absolutely amazed and elated. "Lord, thank You, thank You."

"Look, I said to Alan, I've got my offering, I've got my offering!"

As I held onto the money Alan looked and said, "What are you going to do with that?"

Excitedly I said, "It's my offering; I'm going to give it!"

When he saw how much it was, naturally he protested, "You can't put all that in the offering!"

But my logic said, *"How could I keep any of it?"* It was the immediate answer to my prayer; this money belonged to the Lord. Without considering that we did not have enough petrol in the van to drive home or money for even the basics of life, I put the whole gift into the offering and worshiped the Lord.

Alan had blessed the people with his excellent ministry and was to preach again that evening. We were invited to an elder's home and given a wonderful traditional Sunday roast dinner. The children did not need to be encouraged to eat all they could while they had the opportunity. After the evening meeting we accepted the warm invitation to return home with the family again for supper. In the next thirty minutes our world changed! First, Alan was handed a very generous gift from the church. Our initial thought was, "This is the money for the wood worm treatment. Oh, thank You Lord!" Then, our host wrote a personal gift for us. During this long period of trial we had been praying for money to help Bishwanath who was still in hospital in Bombay. As we looked at the check we knew now we could assist plans that were being made for him to travel to Australia for treatment. Before we got over the joy and thankfulness for these wonderful gifts we were then astounded when we were handed an envelope and inside was cash! This was so amazing. We had been given checks, but we still needed cash to buy the petrol to get us home! The Lord covered every eventuality.

While these miracles were happening, the lady of the house was busy in the kitchen. She suddenly appeared pushing the largest cardboard box imaginable filled with every conceivable grocery item. She said the Lord told her to do this. She had emptied the food from her refrigerator and cleared her pantry shelves and even included toothpaste and toiletries. These items, like breakfast cereals, had become luxuries for us during the past months. Our minds were in a whirl and our hearts were overflowing.

It was late when we left for home but the miles sped by as we filled the air with worship and praise, thanking God for His absolute faithfulness. He knew our every need and He had provided. He had seen our obedience and proved to us that those who "believe will not be put to shame." That night marked the end of seven months of continual trial, the grip of financial lack was broken. As we had observed in the past, it appears that some gifts act like a key; they unlock the flow of finance and stifle the opposition of the enemy. The gift of £200 to me and then my determination to give it away seemed to be the key. Did the deliverance come because the lesson was learnt, or was it in response to the "widow's mite"? We may never know, but one thing is sure, God is no man's debtor.

God provided in abundance for more than our needs. We had money for all the immediate pressing demands and money to give. Within days Alan was offered a very favorable consulting position with a local Christian printing company. We had peace about this knowing that this door had been opened by the Lord. Alan was able to adjust his few working hours to suit ministry demands and the company even paid him generously.

During those painful months that made no sense, God was working deep obedience in us, out of the furnace of trial, through pain, perplexity and patience. He forged yet another level of indomitable faith within us, that was certainly put to the test as during all those days, Alan continued to bleed excessively and no medical treatment brought permanent relief. We were still totally cast on God for his healing; continuing to believe when there appeared to be no hope.

One morning while Alan was alone in the house and bleeding profusely, the Lord visited him. He told him to anoint himself with oil and then declare that he was healed. Alan went to the kitchen and knelt down while bleeding heavily; he anointed himself with cooking oil and believed. It made no sense, nothing changed, he was still bleeding. When I came home, he was holding a blood soaked cloth to his nose as he declared, "I'm healed!" Little did Alan know that another five years of trial would pass before the fruit of his faith, his glorious healing, would be manifested.

CHAPTER 25

PUTTING FAITH TO WORK

A Second Term in India: 1969

The three years in England passed quickly, and we never forgot that the Lord had whispered, "You will return to India in three years." It would have been easy to brush this word aside as we had no invitation or obvious way to return, or clarity as to where we should go. We had become very settled. The children were in school, the church was growing and it hardly seemed the time to leave, but despite it all, we felt compelled to obey the word from the Lord.

Contemplating living in Bombay again prompted us to pray that we should return with a car. To buy one in India was prohibitive those days. The most suitable car to take was the Triumph Herald as spare parts were freely available. We began to pray. We were very precise, "Lord give us a red and white Triumph Herald!" We had no means of buying a car so all we could do was pray, which we did every day; dozens of times a day. We reminded Him and praised Him for the red and white Triumph Herald! My constant declaration became, "Those who believe will not be put to shame." Every day we expected that somehow the car would be delivered to us.

In order to transport the car to India we had to reserve freight space on the ship weeks before we sailed. The instructions from the shipping line were very exact. The reservation required the car model and dimensions. Alan decided to measure a friend's Triumph Herald and then, armed with that information we reserved space to transport the car to India— the car we did not yet possess. "Faith is being sure of what we hope for and certain of what we do not see." (Heb.11:1) Faith changes the way you think. When God whispers something incredible into your heart and you believe it, as we did concerning the car, something miraculous begins to happen.

Prayer that is rooted in faith in God grows out of an intimate, experiential knowledge of Him. Faith is always in something or somebody. For example; you trust the ladders to hold you, or you have faith in your father; your history gives you reason to trust. Faith is not a spiritual faculty that is independent of God where I say, "I have faith it will all work out in the end!" or "I have faith God will heal me." But in reality all you have is knowledge that God heals. Now you need to meet the Healer.

True faith is in the person of the Lord Jesus Christ and each of us through experience with Him develops our own reason for faith in Him. Your trust or faith cannot be dependent upon just the word from a witness, it must move from intellectual knowledge to a knowing in the spirit. Even the word of God is a witness, but that word has to become flesh in us, in other words—it becomes a witness within, we know the word by divine revelation, we experience the word. The word that speaks within produces true faith. The impossible seems perfectly possible; one's thinking is transformed.

To gain this position of faith one has to jump many hurdles. Doubt is always lurking about trying to gain entrance. If doubt is silenced, then there are people who will try to deter you, and always there is 'the waiting', *"Oh Lord when will You answer?"* This is the trial. Faith is contested; but if you endure, if you persist, if you refuse to have second thoughts and look back, but press on undeterred, you will possess whatever treasure the Lord whispers into your heart. What He speaks into being will be manifested.

Then the day arrived; an unknown person called saying they wanted to give us a car! Tentatively we asked what kind of car he had in mind. He went on to describe his red and white Triumph Herald stating that he felt sure the Lord was telling him to donate it to us! We all ran outside to greet him as he drove a red and white miracle into the driveway. Praising God I was declaring, "He who believes will not be put to shame!" Not only did we receive the car, but with it all the money required to ship it to India and get it through customs. Don't ever doubt, "He who believes shall not be put to shame!" We needed signs that the Lord was sending us out again and this tangible evidence was a huge boost to our faith as we sought to follow the Lord like little children.

Eventually the manner of our return became clear, we would go back to Bombay but not to the Gospel Literature Press. Alan had visited various people in India and came to the conclusion that he should find secular work to give our residency legitimacy. With the change in Indian immigration law we did not qualify to apply for a missionary visa. A Hindu man offered Alan a part-time position to help with the modernization of his printing company and armed with that invitation, we arrived in Bombay praying that this would be enough to give us acceptance by immigration.

Standing in the immigration line with our two children, we observed the rigorous questioning that other passengers were having. We stood and prayed. A teacher going to a Christian boarding school that catered to Indian as well as overseas children was refused entry. We thought our reason for entry was very inferior to her's and prayed all the more. Only the Lord could open the way for us, our faith was in His word, "You will return in three years." Our turn came, we stood before the officer and with minimal questioning were waved past and for the second time we entered India.

Not much had changed in three years. Again we were confronted with the great difficulty of finding somewhere to live. Initially we were told about two available rooms and gladly took them as the owner was not demanding *pugery* only to find that the other part of the flat was occupied by prostitutes! We began a nomadic life, staying wherever we could, often in other peoples' homes with our children and few belongings moving from one temporary location to another. Nothing was secure. Eventually we moved into the flat belonging to a mission family who were in New Zealand for six months.

The nation had adopted an anti-missionary attitude and as we did not have missionary visas, we needed to be cautious that our activities didn't attract attention. Alan's 'tent making' was always a cover as well as providing financially for us, but it also meant that he worked two very hard jobs despite continual ill health. The Christian scene in Bombay had changed while we had been in England. New Zealand missionaries were planting vibrant new churches. Some of those we had led into the baptism of the Holy Spirit had so matured that now they were the leaders in the new churches. The Spirit was doing a new exciting thing in the city.

School life in Bombay was very hard for our children. The culture, language and a very different style of teaching proposed huge obstacles for them; they were accustomed to a freer type of education. Most of the other missionaries we knew sent their children to mission boarding schools away in the hills. We had never considered sending our children, but Rachel, then nine years old, wanted to go when she discovered that her friends were going. This forced us to pray and reluctantly we came to the conclusion that this was the Lord's will. Rachel left and Duncan stayed home. She seemed happy but we felt wretched.

On her first visit home she did all she could to persuade her brother to go back to school with her. Now Duncan was only six years old and we had no plans for him to leave, even though he was very unhappy in his day school and becoming unwell with the long days, followed by long bus journeys in temperatures over 100 degrees. Furthermore, we had no money to send him.

The whole question took center stage when one morning, my Bible reading was from 1 Samuel chapter 2 where, I read the passage of Hannah praising the Lord. At first I thought she praised God for the expected child but then, on closer reading, I realized the occasion was when she gave her son to the Lord and left him with Eli! I sat in the old rocking chair and wept as the Lord made it plain to me that Duncan should go back to school with Rachel; I could hardly bear the thought. The school was one thousand miles away in the south of India.

After settling Duncan, my little one in the school dormitory and reluctantly leaving Rachel, I walked back to Brooklands Guest House where all the other mothers would be staying before catching their transport back to far flung places all over India. I slowly wandered through the tea gardens, up the hill singing to myself as I went; sometimes it bubbled over in praise. I said to myself, *"I must be the most unnatural mother, why am I feeling so much joy?"* Then the Lord reminded me of Hannah, she praised God when little Samuel was given to the Lord. Inside the same joy was bursting from me, though it seemed very out of place round the dinner table among a sad group of mothers. The uniform glum expression upon the faces told its own story. There was very little conversation; each mother in her anguished thoughts was re-living their farewells and the moment of leaving their precious children behind.

When I arrived back in Bombay a check was waiting. It was enough to cover all Duncan's school fees. Though it was painful, we had to believe we were in the will of the Lord and He would cause even this to work together for good for all of us.

The following year in 1970 again we needed a place to live. The New Zealand family who had kindly loaned their home was returning. At about the same time, two young men called at the house saying, they had found Christ through a radio program and asked if we would give them weekly Bible teaching. Grenville and his friend lived in a nearby fishing village called Chuim that had been swallowed up in the endless sprawl of the city. It was known for its drunkards, immorality and suicides. On one occasion I had visited the post office near to the village and came home to announce, "I will never go there again, I needed a burka to protect me from all the lecherous eyes!" But the Lord knew what he was doing. Within a week, accommodation was available right in the village and we moved in. We shared the place with rats and many other undesirables! But in that most unlikely place, a wonder began.

Now we understood why the children had to go to boarding school—Chuim was not suitable for them. At night there were drunken brawls in front of our house and the demonized wandered about by day. We were the center of interest; the whole neighborhood knew where the foreigners lived. It became an advantage when we started a church in our home, a central place in the village, many came to look and a few ventured in.

The work was so contended it was evident that our coming had alerted the powers of darkness. We experienced the most bizarre happenings and were even physically assaulted by demons. One Wednesday night Alan and I resorted to continual warring prayer till we eventually felt a breakthrough. Unknown to us at the time, a principality was vanquished; from that day, the pressure was off and the work began to grow.

God works in amazing ways, but so often we do not recognize His hand directing our daily affairs while He accomplishes His purpose. I had become pregnant with David who was later to be born in the Holy Family Hospital. During the prenatal visits I had spoken with a nursing sister who belonged to the Catholic medical mission running the hospital. I discovered she was spiritually hungry and was prompted to give her the book, "The Cross and the Switch Blade" by David Wilkerson. True faith is implicitly obeying divine instructions even when it is only a nudge. I then looked for an opportunity to follow up on our conversation. The opportunity came the day I arrived at the hospital to give birth to David; that day we had plenty of time to talk.

She had been reading about the Catholic Charismatic Renewal in the United States and wondered if such things could happen there in Bombay. She longed to be baptized in the Holy Spirit and asked if Alan would visit the sisters' communal house to teach them what that really meant. Pentecost was coming and in her thinking, it seemed perfect timing if God would give them their personal Pentecost. Alan agreed and had a wonderful evening with about twelve sisters, he prayed for them all. The Lord heard their prayers and saw their hunger. He sent the Holy Spirit and He fell upon them all. History was in the making and nobody knew that a move of God had begun.

From that encounter in the labor room of a maternity hospital, the Spirit came making way for Alan to teach a weekly meeting in the local Catholic school. The effect of the Catholic Charismatic movement, widely influencing the United States, was now being felt in Bombay. The Holy Spirit was quickening His people. A number of priests, sisters and lay people were seeking God gathering in small charismatic groups for teaching and fellowship. When Alan began the Thursday night meetings hundreds came, drawn into the life of the Spirit by the anointing upon his winsome teaching. He taught them how to live a life of faith and what it meant to be born again and to live in the Kingdom of God. He was able to do all this without offending his Catholic hosts who had set up the location and the opportunity. The Lord gave us both favor with the local priests so that we were able to train teams who then went into Catholic institutions in Bombay and then to many places in India. For four years, there was an unhindered opportunity to preach the Gospel. Countless miracles and deliverances took place. An untold number were saved, filled with the Holy Spirit and received the word of God.

The Lord began to answer prayer in a definite way concerning the many local alcoholics. In an area similar to Chuim, where we lived, was an infamous street, Chapel Road. Most of the men were without work and spent their days drinking, gambling and in every kind of wickedness. One of these men, Carlton, was delivered from drinking when he was powerfully saved. He seemed to be getting on fine, but coming to meetings was not enough; no one had made time to personally disciple him. Though apparently steady, four months later we all had a horrible shock—he had slipped back again into the lifestyle of drunkenness.

The Lord used Carlton's backsliding to awaken everyone, even the new believers to a more loving concern for each other. Some of the local Christians went out looking for Carlton in the streets and drinking houses. Their concern caused other alcoholics to be interested enough to come to the Thursday Meeting where Alan was teaching. We all praised God when nine of them sought the Lord, with deep earnestness—the Holy Spirit was at work. That evening they were saved and delivered, needless to say, we all became practiced at casting out devils!

Alan went to one of the village houses and had a Bible study with these men. They went and found Carlton in the street and persuaded him to come also. What a merciful God we serve! The Holy Spirit fell upon Carlton and completely delivered him; he was restored and danced for joy. He went on to be a faithful servant of the Lord leading many to salvation and effectively teaching the word.

The following evening we returned to the same group and our hearts were filled with gratitude to see the wonderful thing God had done.

They continued to stand together encouraging one another. Years later we met with many of them again. They were now stable family men, loving their wives, caring for their children, and many had become leaders in the church, passionately following the Lord.

These miracles remind me of a vision the Lord gave me during those months. I saw a hand go into filthy muck but it came out clean, holding a glorious sparkling jewel. These men were the jewels rescued from the deepest pit of hell. We prayed that they would be as pure as He is pure and shine with the glory of Jesus in that very dark place. The Catholic charismatic work continued to grow into the tens of thousands. Many of the converts found life in new fellowships and today, the church in the city of Bombay owes much to this movement.

While the Holy Spirit was doing miraculous things among the Catholics, the church we had planted was also growing. The new believers were being established in a faith that can move mountains and pull down strongholds. It was normal for these new Christians to take God at His Word, act upon it and see prayers answered. The challenges of Bombay life were enough to bring any Christian to their knees.

The continual need among the congregation was for accommodation and jobs which gave plenty of room for exercising faith. The shortage of accommodation affected everyone including those waiting to marry. As a church, we took a stand in prayer to ask God to release accommodation to everyone in need in the fellowship. Again and again we saw miracles of provision without paying pugery. In a society where there was 30 percent unemployment, the whole church shared the heartache together till we came to a position in faith where everyone employable had a job. God showed Himself strong on our behalf. The lessons in faith that we had painfully learned through many a trial were now producing fruit in dozens of others' lives.

The many new believers created a need for leadership training and the production of teaching materials. Trinity Fellowship was formed; an organization which published "Outpouring", a teaching magazine to help establish the new converts and train the new leaders in both the Catholic movement and our own church sphere of influence. I became the editor and continued to work with it even after we returned to England. As this was happening new churches were being planted in many places in Bombay and we began to see the prayers prayed during the days in the Baptist church being answered. Our 'struggle meetings' as I had called them, were now bearing fruit; the spirit of revival was in the air.

Alan's teaching gift had matured and was greatly appreciated. This led to invitations to many mission stations all over India and in Nepal. In our travels we had the unusual privilege of ministering to missionaries as well as the local people. Fortunately David, our baby was a born traveler and seemed to enjoy the endless journeys and the variety of situations we encountered. All this wider ministry was accomplished at the same time as keeping up the momentum of the work in Bombay.

There were times when I stayed home and Alan traveled alone. But let me share with you from a letter I wrote describing my days while Alan was gone.

"I would like to tell you how my time has gone these few days with Alan away. First of all, there was Neelu, a Sindhi Hindu, the wife of a Naval commander, who we had casually met on the train coming back from Mussoorie. She was in Bombay for just two weeks. I had invited her over for lunch and with very little difficulty was able to lead her to Christ. She was so open and longing for Jesus. I then prayed for her to be filled with the Spirit and she literally danced for joy round the flat. We have put her in touch with some people in Delhi where she lives.

The next day a woman named Agnes, from Chuim, visited me with her sister Sophe. You will understand how thrilled I was to have somebody from Chuim village come to us after all this time. These women told me a fantastic story concerning evil spirits, mediums and strange manifestations that would make even a Hitchcock thriller seem tame. Sophe's husband seems to be a very powerful medium and has been able to deceive his family and relatives. Both these women received Jesus as their Lord and Savior. Agnes came again the following day bringing with her Marina, Sophe's daughter. With a little explanation Marina also received the Lord. You can imagine it was me dancing round the room this time!"

The growth of the work in the church had been consistent and amazing to us. The city was ready to hear the word of God so that it was easy to witness and lead people to the Lord. The majority of the congregation were baptized in the Holy Spirit and manifested it through their supernatural lives. Not surprisingly the church was known for healings, deliverances and transformed lives. The power of the Holy Spirit led the new believers to love the Word. Soon there was a new level of faith among them as they too learned that true faith is implicitly obeying divine instructions. Operation Mobilization had teams in the city and tirelessly evangelized by every means. Passionate people prayed; the numbers were not many but they truly expected revival fire to fall. In those early days we never dreamed that years later thousands of churches would be planted in Bombay and besides Catholics finding Christ in His fullness, countless Hindus and Muslims would also follow Him.

CHAPTER 26

LIFE ON THE MOVE

In September 1973, after a few months in England to introduce our new son David to our families, we were back again in Bombay. As we hunted for accommodation, this time God provided a fine apartment in a good neighborhood.

At the culmination to a happy few weeks with the children home from boarding school, we arranged our first meeting in our wonderful new home hosting a special evening event. We had an attractive card printed and invited everyone from the twenty-two flats in the building. Other Christian friends were invited only on the condition they brought an unconverted friend. By the end of the evening more than seventy people packed into our large room for an informal time in which the gospel was presented through powerful testimonies. A Hindu graduate who had come to Christ a week earlier, though nervous, spoke boldly of her new-found faith. That evening seven were saved including an older Hindu woman who, we were later told, yielded to Christ on the bus going home.

While the children were in boarding school we were busy travelling to the far reaches of the Indian subcontinent. A British missionary invited Alan for evangelistic meetings in Madras that he hoped would build the small, new English-speaking assembly. At first the nominal Christian congregation was very complacent, only 'enjoying good meetings', but completely unresponsive to the call of the Spirit for sacrificial living. It was four days later before liberty came into the services and the Lord began to save; by the end of the week whole families had been united in Christ and a remarkable number of old people had wept their way to the Savior. During the week, the sick were prayed for and God healed many. It became a time of wonders and outstanding miracles! A man came and sat on the front seat asking for prayer. The problem was, he wanted to see, but only had an empty eye socket. I stood behind him while Alan, standing in front of the man, laid his hand over the empty socket while he called out in faith for a creative miracle. I shall never forget the look of delight and astonishment upon Alan's face when he lifted his hand; there looking back at him was a brand new eye! With equal joy, a deaf and dumb Hindu woman acted like a delighted child as she heard for the first time! Before we left Madras, Alan spoke at a pastors' meeting where fifty were gathered, and then to two thousand assembled for a night of prayer. Madras in those days was very much more Christian compared to Bombay where perhaps twenty might gather for our prayer nights.

We planned for a prolonged time of travelling while the children were in boarding school. Once back in Bombay we had just five days to arrange for visas, health documents and air reservations in readiness for our journey north. When we thought all was done, Indian Airlines cancelled their timetable the day before we were due to leave! Very aware that as Alan would say, "Our Heavenly Father 'owned' Indian Airlines", we set off to find that He had provided seats for us on the most convenient flight. That story was repeated many times and kept us on schedule all the way.

En route, we had fruitful meetings in Delhi and Patna with the Roman Catholics. In the Catholic Hospital in Patna we met a Jesuit priest from Jamshedpur. He said that for some time the brothers of his order had been seeking God for the power of the Holy Spirit but had got nowhere. Being discouraged, the meetings had dwindled but never quite stopped. He had been told of Alan's ministry among Catholics in Bombay and wished to meet him, but had no idea how to contact him. Imagine his surprise when we walked into the hospital ward where he had been a patient for the past two months. He was due for discharge the following day; how perfect is the Lord's timing! This divinely appointed contact led some months later to Alan being invited to teach at a retreat for Jesuit priests.

Travelling with children has its own set of extra challenges. This journey brought us to the Nepali border ministering in another Mission church setting. When we arrived at the home where we were to stay the parents told us their children had measles! We were at the beginning of an extensive mission tour and to think of David contracting measles was a daunting prospect. We prayed. Here was another opportunity to exercise the prayer of faith. God heard us; David never developed measles and was healthy for the whole journey.

On another occasion while staying in an inhospitable place, David, became extremely jaundiced. His skin was dark yellow. Again we realized this kind of life demanded that we know Jesus as healer. We prayed in faith and believed David would be healed. Then I asked him if he was hungry and to my surprise he said, "Yes, can I have fried egg and chips?" Knowing that fried food was the last thing to give to someone with jaundice, but believing that he was healed, even though he was still yellow, I gave him egg and chips. Next day he was well and his color had returned.

After a difficult journey, we arrived in Kathmandu, Nepal where we spent a delightful few hours. Alma Hagen, a seasoned Nepali missionary, took us to see the city which is unlike anything we had ever seen before; a place packed with temples and many interesting sights. In baskets evenly balanced on the either end of bamboo poles across their shoulders, men carried heavy loads of every conceivable thing, including a dead pig. Hippies openly smoked 'pot' in the bazaar area and Alan was asked if he wanted his ears cleaned by a professional ear cleaner!

Despite all the temples and outward appearance of idolatry we found the Nepali people to be most friendly and open. There was not the spiritual hostility we had expected. We couldn't help but compare Kathmandu with Patna, which we had just left. There the spiritual opposition was blatant. Students were rioting and burning shops and we were shouted at by a mob of young men in a frenzy of idol worship. In Nepal the authorities were against Christ, but in Patna and other places in India it seemed the people were against Him. The evening meeting in Kathmandu was a glorious time with the heavens opened. It was an opportunity to meet many people who before were just names on a prayer list.

The next day we were on the move again and were met at the little air strip at Pokhra and so began nine days of ministry to the missionaries, workers and local folk connected with the International Nepal Fellowship. At that time Pokhra was the second largest place in Nepal with a population of 20,000, much larger than we had expected. There was a good bazaar with electric street lights, limited water supply and even a bus service of sorts from one end of the town to the other.

We had meetings with the patients at Green Pastures Leprosarium and were deeply impressed by the sight of so many maimed and hopeless individuals sitting to hear the Word of God. One usually associates lepers with beggars. In contrast, we saw the powerful emancipating force of the gospel in the lives of former patients, well dressed with their families having the joy of the Lord on their faces. These were now mainly employed by the hospital.

There were many wonderful conversions during those few days. Outsiders and church contacts came and soon ripples of blessing were being felt in many places. We were then on the move again, this time to Shining Hospital, where the meetings continued. Many trekked long distances to be present. Patients and staff from Green Pastures swelled the Nepali meetings to overflowing. Graciously, the Lord saved souls, filled others with the Holy Spirit and dealt with church leaders bringing healing and reconciliations. Both of us were given very apt messages and great liberty in preaching. We had a lot of personal counseling to do and praised God for the word of wisdom and knowledge which soon revealed problems and gave answers.

Following a powerful week, and without a break, we were on the road Sunday afternoon back to Kathmandu and then on to Bhuksa, a small place in the hills near to the Indian-Bhutan border.

After days on the train and hours in a vehicle we came to the end of the road. It had been exhausting, full of frustrations and endless waits so we were relieved to see the coolies waiting for us ready to carry our belongings up the mountain. This last leg of the journey meant that we had to climb 3000 ft. walking 4 miles through jungle paths. We climbed and clambered over rocks up the twisting path through the undergrowth.

After about an hour the sun was on our backs and it was hot. David, only two years old, had been happy to scramble as best he could for a short way, but then Alan carried him on his shoulders making slow, steady progress up the continual gradient.

During the previous months Alan's bleeding had noticeably diminished so that now it was unusual if he bled; this respite soon had its rewards with him having more energy. All the time we believed for a manifestation of the complete healing that we knew was his and deliberately stayed strong in faith when suddenly, he would bleed again. I would hope and pray that it wasn't the beginning of another spate of trouble. That morning on the Bhutan border I climbed up the path behind Alan singing for joy and giving thanks. I was witnessing a wonder; Alan, walking up a mountain carrying David! That day I knew he was healed. Alan's faith was vindicated. For five years he had stood in faith declaring that he was healed regardless of the continual bleeding. He believed the word the Lord had spoken to him in England all those years before; his persistence and dogged faith was wonderfully rewarded. Alan continued to gain weight and regain health. God manifested his complete healing; the prayers of many were answered.

Living along the border were scattered communities of Hindu Nepalese and Buddhist Bhutanese. They tended to live in separate villages. We had been invited by Hellin Hukka Dukpa, a Finnish missionary, married to the Bhutanese pastor of the local church with whom we stayed. Hellin ran a small dispensary on her verandah through which she had contact with people from a very wide area. Medical care in those remote districts was non-existent.

I could hear Alan preaching to the patients on the verandah. The Lord alerted me to the immense strength of the demonic power in the area. I prayed and had assurance that God was going to do an amazing work; He would come in healing power if Alan prayed for the sick. The first to respond for salvation was a Hindu man who had been politically active and had threatened Hellin's life. Now he was sick with tuberculosis and she was the only one who could help him. Compelled to come for treatment he made his peace with her but wonder of wonders, that day he was healed and made his peace with God!

Many of the people had goiters. I saw one woman with a growth in her neck the size of a baby's head. Two patients came with snake bites, their bloated limbs throbbing with poison. As Alan prayed, he watched the swollen arm go down before his eyes. Hellin was often confronted with conditions that were impossible for her to handle, but the Lord caused her simple remedies and prayer of faith to bring healing to many.

The week was packed with meetings. Originally the invitation had been for a Pastors' Conference, but the evangelistic opportunity was obvious. Alan said he felt like a preaching machine! We were both continually busy. We began with a pastors meeting at 8:00 am, at 10:00 am a Nepali meeting and so it continued all day and sometimes there were two meetings at once for the different language groups! I did one and Alan did the other. When the electricity failed we were very thankful for a rest, otherwise further meetings would have been arranged! The people were so thrilled to have a visiting speaker; they walked long distances through the mountains and stayed all week to listen.

Although our time in Buksa was tiring we were filled with joy; so many came to Christ including three of Hellin's own household. We were invited to preach in a Hindu village where there were no Christians. With David, we set off through the leech infested jungle for a two mile walk, returning only after dark and just in time to take the Bhutanese meeting! Before I could go into the house I stripped off my sari and pulled dozens of leeches off my legs and feet. But it was all worth it; so many people had been saved!

It was time to leave. We would cross a river on our way down the mountain, so a hurried baptismal service was arranged where thirteen people each gave testimony before going down into the frigid water. One old Buddhist woman said she was the first in her house to come to Christ. What a victory! But, what a price she would have to pay. She asked for prayer for the rest of her family. Many more baptisms followed in the next weeks for those unable to come down to the river that morning.

The pastors had been spiritually cold and discouraged when they arrived. In the meetings we were working with translators so at first it was difficult for us to know just what was happening and how the congregation was responding; but now there was no doubt. God had done a great work in those remote hills that now echoed with singing and praise.

Making our way back down the mountainside we were greeted at each Christian house along the way and given oranges, bananas or cucumbers. Ishmael, one of the pastors, received a freshly boiled piece of pork which was uncomfortably hot in his hand. As we walked down and down we were amazed that we had ever walked up; it was so steep.

The next leg of the journey took us to Darjeeling. A small group of Christian workers were gathered and the Lord ministered to them. On the Sunday morning Alan preached in Pastor Ishmael's church. Many were saved including a husband and wife. A young man from Sikkim and another from Bhutan were filled with the Holy Spirit and a woman from Czechoslovakia in a tragic situation found Jesus to be her peace. They were wonderful days. The Lord certainly anointed Alan to do the work of an evangelist; we had such expectancy for souls in every place.

Traveling has its blessings as well as its hardships. Whilst crammed into trains or waiting at airports we were able to have so many revealing conversations which opened the way to speak to hungry hearts.

One woman said, "And how did you meet Christ?"

A young Italian world traveler said, "Yes, the present world is only a magnification of the mess of individual lives. A new birth is essential."

"This is wonderful news. Why don't you go to all our villages, to the sad and the sinners and those behind bars? All need to know this," added a Hindu businessman.

The need in Nepal during those early pioneering days called us back again and again. An invitation came for us to visit Tansen where a mission hospital had been established and run by some remarkable women. With David we set out on the long journey wondering what we would encounter this time, well aware that the Nepali government did not permit evangelizing and making converts. When we arrived it had been arranged for Alan to speak to small groups of staff and patients at the hospital. At the Saturday evening meeting were those who had never heard the gospel, who asked for further instruction so Alan spent Sunday afternoon telling the gospel from A-Z to different groups of enquirers. Three, who had had longer contact with the gospel, came through to salvation and a few others were filled with the Spirit. Others went away convinced but not committed. Nothing is done in a hurry in Nepal.

Traveling always has its interesting side. We left Tansen at 6:00 a.m. with a coolie carrying our heavy case. David sat on Alan's shoulders as we walked quickly for 20-25 minutes down to the bus. We passed the village pump where women were washing clothes, collecting water or bathing themselves. The doors of the homes were all open as we passed along the village streets; food was being cooked, the morning chores had begun, but all work stopped just to watch us pass by.

When we got to the bus it was already crammed full. People squashed up on every seat and dozens standing inside with an equal number trying to get in! As I was about to join the crush, I was beckoned round to the driver's side. There next to the driver a small stool was placed for me. Clasping David, I quickly sat on it as the bus was about to go. Alan went to look for the coolie. About ten long minutes elapsed before he eventually appeared with our case which Alan then hauled up onto the roof of the bus and all was set. Alan too, clambered up onto the bus by the driver's door. Someone kindly made space for him. Seven hours later we were in Pokhra, after covering only a distance of about seventy miles!

Back in Bombay the work among the Catholics continued powerfully on many fronts. The converts were so zealous they went everywhere preaching the gospel and doing the works of Jesus. A miraculous thing was taking place; the very atmosphere of the area was being changed.

Jesus was the talking point; the questions continuously asked were, "Do you know Jesus?"

"Have you received the Holy Spirit?"

The spirit of revival was in the air, churches were growing and many Christians were taking a stand for Christ even in situations that invited persecution.

Alan had continued teaching the Thursday Meeting for four years until there was a concern among the Catholic hierarchy that the people were being disaffected from the Catholic church; it was true that a number had left the Catholic church for other congregations. The Catholic bishop visited the Thursday Meeting and shortly afterwards the meetings were abruptly brought to an end to the consternation of many. This prompted even more to leave the Catholic church but others stayed and gathered the hungry ones into classes.

During those four years of teaching, hundreds of Bibles had been distributed; thousands of lives changed forever and wonderful friendships forged. Many of the converts became powerful leaders, planting churches and evangelizing in some very difficult places. We never ceased to be amazed at their enthusiastic zeal for Christ.

Our time in India was drawing to a close. Rachel had already left for England and was staying with a family while she completed her tenth year in school. We had lived in Bombay over a period of thirteen life-changing years, but now the Lord was clearly leading us to settle back in England and create stability for our children, who had also sacrificed for the Gospel. Over the years they had lived through many difficulties that were normal for the children of missionaries, but we were acutely aware that they had paid a price. God is no man's debtor and we always believed that they would be abundantly blessed.

In 1976 a phase of life came to an end. We finally left India and returned to live in England. Though we left India's soil, we could not leave India; she had entwined herself in our hearts so that for the last 50 years we have retained relationships and continued to return for ministry.

CHAPTER 27

FAITH VINDICATED

Home in England 1976

A miracle occurred before we left India so that when we returned to our home in England it was completely paid for. The mortgage on the property had been fixed at a low interest rate, but then inflation had driven interest rates three times higher. The mortgage company, wishing to rid themselves of a loss making mortgage, wrote saying that they required us to accept a new mortgage arrangement with a far higher interest rate or pay off the existing mortgage in full. We were unable to meet their impossible options; it was obvious the company just wished to be free from the contract. We had no answer and it seemed we were in danger of losing the property. At that time The Elms was home for a long term mission family of six from India, and we could not think of asking them to leave. We had no idea what to do other than lay the whole problem before the Lord and wait, confident that we were in the center of the Lord's will. We trusted God. He was faithful; we knew He would see us through this trial as he had done so many times before. He had the answer; He was the God of the impossible.

My mind went back to the emotional moment as I shut the door of The Elms and walked away that snowy morning in February 1963. When we left to go to India I was remembering saying under my breath, "Lord, I'm leaving it to You, You look after the house." Over the years God kept us in faith. He provided the right tenants and the necessary finance year after year. As we were now confronted with this new situation, there was nothing we could do but trust 'the Lord who does all things well'. Continually praying, we waited to see what He would do. When there is nothing you can do about a situation, all you can do is to pray and wait!

Some days later we received a letter from a company of solicitors in England. "Look at this. Look at this!" Alan said, holding the letter out for me to see. Reading it out loud we learned that we were beneficiaries in the will of an anonymous donor. To this day we do not know who it was. We were to receive an inheritance that would amount to just nine pounds short of everything needed to pay off the mortgage!

Sweltering in Bombay's monsoon, hearing the usual cries from the street, it seemed that nothing had changed; but with that letter, everything had changed. We were now the owners of our own home in England. It was hard to believe. How we praised God. We thanked and praised Him again and again. His answer to our prayers was amazing. Again He made it clear, "Those who believe will not be put to shame"!

Some months later when we arrived home and came to our familiar front door, we were again filled with gratitude for the gift that had made it possible and to our faithful Father who watched over every detail of the walk of faith that had brought us here. After thirteen years away with others using our home, He paid for it in full and then gave it back to us as a gift. God is so good! He is kind, He is loving; the gift of our home totally overwhelmed us.

Rachel was now sixteen and in her final two years at school in preparation for university, and Duncan, at thirteen years was experiencing for the first time what it meant to live in England. David nearly five was ready to start school. The transition was not easy for the children or for us. Alan again led the small church where we had worked before; it gave us joy as it grew rapidly in numbers and life.

The Church scene had changed during the years we had been away. The Charismatic movement had birthed many new churches with very different ways of function and many new influential leaders. Alan visited various leadership groups as he tried to find where he would fit in. Soon he was invited to join an apostolic team where he became one of the main Bible teachers. Alan immersed himself in the new relationships and wide open doors of ministry. At times he would return to India for prolonged visits or travel in the then Communist East European nations teaching and evangelizing in difficult places.

My time now moved from pioneering in India to being centered in the home. The ministry demands upon Alan meant that I was often alone. One Saturday morning, as I washed the kitchen floor having just said goodbye to Alan for another weekend away, and another weekend alone for me, I complained to the Lord. I have never forgotten His response. With great clarity the Lord said to me, "He is another man's servant." That has stayed with me for the rest of my life as I have always tried to assist him to fulfill his calling and as his wife "to do him good all the days of my life."

No longer were we being tested financially. Now the trials of faith were more inward as the Lord graciously continued His perfecting work in my heart. I found the British church life challenging with its restrictions upon women; it seemed to hold little of the freedom and joy I had experienced ministering in India. Deep in my heart I longed for India. One day the Lord confronted me, "Your feet are here, but your heart is in India." I knew that was true. Sadly it had taken me three years to come to this understanding. I repented: I had resisted His will for this time in my life. By faith I determined to live joyfully and fulfill my calling in this new environment.

While Alan was away on one of his ministry visits to India, the church at home planned a baptismal service. As I was putting David, our youngest to bed, he said he wanted to be baptized with the other candidates on Sunday. He protested, "I am a Christian!" I tried to persuade him that it would be best to wait till Daddy came home. Sitting up in bed, he made it clear that he was not very happy to wait, he wanted to be baptized.

To console him I said, "Well, we can pray that you be baptized in the Holy Spirit."

His childish response was, "Goody, goody, let's do that one then!"

I shall never forget this precious little four year old sitting up in his bed as I laid my hands upon him. He laughed, cried and spoke in tongues all at once as the Holy Spirit fell upon him in power. I was overwhelmed as I watched the Holy Spirit pouring upon David. When I regained my composure and recognized the power of what was happening, I said, "Let us pray again for your hearing." While still in India we had become aware that David had a measure of hearing impairment, but since being in England we had discovered the full extent of his difficulty. His was a congenital problem with no known treatment. His hearing was poor in both ears to the extent that he required hearing aids. To compensate he had become an efficient lip reader. I laid my hands on David a second time and immediately his ears opened. Now both of us were beside ourselves with joy, laughing and crying all at once. David could hear!

The following day my mind was bombarded with thoughts about people losing their healing. I wondered what I had to do to make sure that wouldn't happen to David. I became quite anxious and felt very responsible; then I understood the enemy was stealing my joy and undermining my faith. I had to deliberately take a stand against doubt and fear. When we are emotionally involved with the healing it appears that our faith is more vulnerable to this kind of attack.

A few days later my faith was again sorely tested. The school nurse had done a routine hearing examination of new children and she sent David home with a letter informing me that he needed to see a specialist as his hearing was deficient. I was shocked; I was convinced that he was healed, but that did not prevent me wondering and hoping that David wasn't losing his healing. The enemy of faith was persistent! Next morning I asked his class teacher why the nurse had sent the letter. I should not have worried, I should have kept my faith but I was still learning. She said the nurse knew that David had had problems so although she found no irregularities in his hearing she sent the letter to cover herself!

Many months later on a routine follow up visit to the Doctor, I was confronted with the rational, unbelieving mind that would not believe that God heals, even when the evidence is before them. When the Doctor saw David's hearing test results which were normal, he said, "Have you bought the same child here?" When I said yes and returned the hearing aids, saying, "He has been healed by Jesus" he was angry. Raising his voice he told me to go and we never went back!

New avenues of ministry opened up for Alan. He became one of the main speakers at the Downs Bible Week, a camp which ministered to tens of thousands in the new churches being established in the days of the charismatic renewal. He continued to travel to many nations as well as return to India again and again. Alan's prophetic teaching gift drew hungry people from far and wide. We planted churches in West Hertfordshire where the firmly established faith principles we had learned formed the foundation of our church life.

Alan continued his ministry to many nations, but most frequently, going to India. He would often be gone for prolonged periods. It was during this time that a deep relationship was forged with John Babu, from Armoor in the state of Andhra Pradesh. John, an alcoholic police officer, had been miraculously converted from Hinduism. Now he was leading a struggling Pentecostal church in a small town called Armoor. One night he had a dream in which he saw a European couple, the woman was dressed in a sari and he noted the details of the man's clothing. The Lord said to John that he should go to Bombay and he would meet these people and he was to submit his ministry to this tall English man. For John to even think of traveling all the way to Bombay was impossible, he barely had enough money to feed his eight children once a day. After a few days, a young missionary couple, passing through the area arrived at his church and said they were on their way to Bombay and offered to take John. With one of his sons, he made the long journey. John was without a change of clothes but would just wash them at night and wear them again the next day. He was poor, but amazingly open to God; truly his riches were in heaven.

Amazingly he was brought right to a conference where Alan and I were ministering, along with another visitor from England. As soon as he saw us, he recognized Alan, and I was wearing the sari he had seen; he knew we were the people in his dream. He said nothing about the dream but watched and prayed while soaking up everything he could learn. He had transitioned from Hinduism to the position of church pastor without training or mentoring from anyone and there was plenty that was new to him.

When it came time for the delegates to leave, John asked Alan if he would visit his church. It was not many months later that Alan made the journey again to India to be with John. The living conditions were very primitive but Alan was not one to complain or to require a certain living standard before he would go. Our practice was always to live indigenously and in the people's homes where possible. That visit was the turning point for the church. Alan taught on the Kingdom of God and began to explain how the church should be founded and believers live. Unfortunately, the 140 people soon dwindled to 40 when they heard the true message of the gospel of the Kingdom and John was dismayed. Alan assured him that now he had a core group of people who meant to follow Christ and that the church would grow and be strong. These many years later demonstrates how true those words have been. The work is called Sion Fellowship and since John's death, is led by John's eldest son, Mohan Babu with over 60,000 members.

From the beginning, John moved in an amazing gift of miracles. Blind eyes were opened, the deaf heard, the demonized were set free, as well as four documented cases of people being raised from the dead. Sion Fellowship has always been known for signs and wonders, it's faith and simple obedience to the Word of God.

Alan continued travelling to India, but primarily to Sion Fellowship and to this day is recognized as the apostolic father to the work. He is loved and honored for his many years of sacrificial input into peoples' lives and into the building of the church. Now the work extends across the state of Andhra to many towns and villages. Tens of thousands of Hindus have been saved and filled with the Holy Spirit, so that the ministry of signs and wonders continues. Mighty leaders have been raised and hundreds of churches planted.

God has given us wonderful encouragement through the lives and ministry of mature, godly, sons in the Lord, who carry on the work in exemplary ways. Today is India's day; the church is growing at a vigorous rate and a generation is rising up who carry the seeds of revival, faith and radical obedience. They will die for Christ, rather than deny Him, and sadly, we are moving steadily into the days when many more may well face that challenge. Some think they live in nations where such persecution will never happen. The days could come even to where you live, and then if confronted with the same challenge, may we not shrink back in fear, but like the first Methodists under the leadership of John Wesley, always be ready to pray, to preach or to die!

CHAPTER 28

FINAL THOUGHTS

Musings on Faith or Folly

Having read these true stories you may feel "Well, they must have been mad!" At times I have had the same thought, but it brought me to consider, what is it that makes some people prepared to embrace sacrifice and even endanger their lives, like Elizabeth Elliott? She stayed with her small child among the Auka Indians, after they had murdered her husband. Madness? Yes many would have said so, but the results were miraculous with a glorious breakthrough for the Kingdom of God into a totally un-evangelized tribal region.

Over the years I have been an avid reader of missionary biographies and many, perhaps most, are stories of adventure, daring, hardship and faith. True acts of faith, which are in response to God's 'rhema' word, will lead to adventure because His plans are God sized! They rarely fit into what we consider normal. True acts of faith are for the daring, without that willingness to step beyond your own comfort zone and rationale, you will never walk in faith. Faith requires that you push into the unknown but at the same time have an answer for others who will legitimately want to advise you; parents, pastors and friends. You must also answer to yourself, is this questionable plan something to satisfy my own desires, or is this of God? It is essential to pass this test; we must know that regardless of the seemingly reckless plan, it is of God. The time will come when that position will be challenged, you must know you are following the plan of God.

Hardship for some is not having a comfortable chair to sit in, but for those intent on going where God sends them, their measure will be, being stoned and left for dead and then getting up and going back into the city! Hardship tests all who would follow the Lord; it is always part of the walk of faith and can be guaranteed to turn up when we embark upon our faith venture. Adventure can be alluring for the young, but it can soon turn to hardship when the whole business of just living takes over. Then, discipline is a most valuable asset. Coupled with determination, it will help even the inexperienced to stay the course. Hardship for the missionary and Christian worker comes in many guises; sickness, lack of finance, disappointment, relational problems, sense of failure, no fruit in the work, feeling that you are wasting your time, and so much more.

Are people born with the ability that will withstand that list of hardships and are fearless when confronted with situations that most of us would shun? Are some born courageous and ready for challenging assignments? The Bible says God has foreordained good works for us to walk in, so that gives me the security that the Lord has designed us for the tasks that He calls us to do. Certainly, God in His magnificent creation did not make us all the same. In most families there is one who would push the envelope, who would cause parents to think, "What will he do next? That child needs an extra guardian angel!"

It is no surprise that these traits are often found in the very people called to do some dangerous or unusual things for the Lord. We had one such child. He knew no fear. At two years old he would jump off the high diving board or into deep water and expect to be fished out by father or anyone else nearby! He was found crawling along a parapet of our ninth floor flat in Bombay. It seems to me that some people are born with the 'dare devil' personality seeing only the adventure, but not the danger. They appear to have no fear. The scraped knees or broken arms are all par for the course for those children who have that driving passion to go where no one else has been. This same driving force takes some people to venture where man has never trod. These focused people are often marked by determination which can be nothing other than stubbornness till it is sanctified.

Apparently as a small child I began my adventures when almost two years old. When my younger sister was being born in the bedroom upstairs, I was clambering onto the coal shed in the garden. Fortunately I did not break any bones as I jumped onto the concrete below causing a panic as the midwife, Miss Thornton, rushed downstairs to check me out. In my school years the adventurous spirit led me to escapades of which I am not proud and would have landed me in a lot of trouble if I had been caught!

Disappointment at not being able to go to France with the school group when I was fifteen years old set in motion a determined plan. I decided that once I was working and as soon as I earned enough money whenever that would be, I would go to France. My monthly salary as a student nurse was barely sufficient to cover basic necessities such as toothpaste and perhaps an occasional family visit, but I was determined; I would go to France. With this goal in view, I carefully budgeted every penny and then quite recklessly planned to go by myself at the first possible opportunity; that came at the end of my first year's training. Few people had been able to venture abroad in those early post war days and even fewer had passports. I set about making plans and saving whatever I could from my meager allowance. After contacting my French pen friend, all was arranged. I would take the ferry to France and catch the train to Paris where I would be met and then stay with a family I didn't know.

Armed with my new passport and a ham sandwich, I took the ferry on a very stormy Easter weekend. The English Channel can be notoriously rough and that day it seemed to be doing its worst. I had never had an occasion to face sea sickness, but that day I understood what it meant! I went onto the deck fascinated by the huge waves. The sea was violent. I took out my ham sandwich and planned to eat my lunch, but all about me were green looking people!

When we disembarked all I heard was French and I knew my school French would not take me far. Squashing all my fears, alone and only seventeen years old, I was so excited. I was in France; my dream had come true. Although I didn't really enjoy my time away, I felt the greatest satisfaction with an ambition fulfilled. I had done it!

Within the personality mix of the adventurous there is, as I have said, a strong dose of determination which takes a lot of wise handling by parents and church leaders. Mission opportunities in today's world call for great works of faith and incredible courage in the face of possible persecution. The genuine calling of God appeals to the adventurous spirit, but the response to that call, requires raw obedience, and that can be very costly. At the same time living the call is the only thing that can wholly satisfy.

Once when life was hard the Lord showed me my cross that I must take up every day. It was padded with soft velvet! It was beautiful; as Jesus said, so easy and so light. I was brought to tears as I thought of our Savior's cross. In that brief moment I was overwhelmed by the abundance of grace and help that is available to us through radical obedience. For the called, walking the road of obedience brings joy and the fullness of satisfaction that can be found in no other place.

Every learned principle of faith becomes the foundation for the next lesson, and so through the years we have the glorious opportunity and privilege to grow in faith. Even today after walking with the Lord for over fifty years, there are still times when I am challenged by my lack of faith. Each of us needs to have the ambition that till we meet the Lord face to face, we will continue to unlock the treasures of faith through a life of radical obedience.

Author Contact Information
And Ministry Resources

Outpouring Missions International
12702 Cimarron Path, Suite 105
San Antonio, TX 78249

Phone: (210) 558-0755
Websites: www.outpouringministries.org
www.cityreachers.net

Log on for Additional Audio Messages by Eileen Vincent Including:

Revival Now God's Way
Warriors NOW
How to Rule When the Enemy is Boss

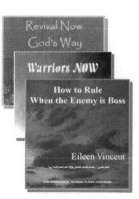

Additional Best Selling Books by Eileen Vincent:

I Will Heal Their Land
The Moving of God's spirit in South Africa
God Can Do it Here
Build Faith for a Glorious Revival Right Where You Live
Something's Happening
Faith to Embrace the Outpouring of the Holy Spirit
No Sacrifice Too Great
The lives of pioneer missionaries CT Studd & Priscilla

Extensive teaching collection available on-line.